TRAIN DRIVER

A Railway Career Memoir

by Roger Taylor

A picture of the author in the cab of a South Australian Alco 830-class hood locomotive, whilst acting as an observer, on the evening staff train from Islington Workshops to Mitcham, during a brief return visit to Australia in March 1978.

COVER PHOTOS

FRONT COVER: The author is seen in the driver's seat of preserved English Electric class forty locomotive after the arrival in London Liverpool Street of the Silver Jubilee Railtour on 22nd January 2005

REAR COVER: The South Australian East-West Express, with 908 at the head, passes through the rural setting of Virginia, 20 3/4 miles north of Adelaide, having just picked up the Electric Staff for the next section whilst heading north to Port Pirie.

CIP data
A catalogue record for this book is available from the British Library

Roger Taylor has asserted his rights to be identified as the author of this work. All illustrations in this book are by the author unless otherwise credited.

From the publishers of

 **BRITISH RAILWAY MODELLING**

Warners Group Publications Plc.,
The Maltings, West Street, Bourne, Lincolnshire PE10 9PH
Phone: 01778 391027 • Fax: 01778 425437

CONTENTS

Dedicated to my wife, Janet, who was very patient during the preparation of this book's manuscript.

FOREWORD

I have known Roger since his arrival at Stratford in 1970. At that time I was a driver and Trade Union representative for the Associated Society of Locomotive Engineers & Firemen (ASLEF), Stratford, East London.

Roger has written a book, full of interest to both railwayman and rail enthusiast. Not many will have had the opportunity, together with the ability and knowledge, to write about their experiences working on both Australian and Britain's railways; Roger has managed to capture both. Details of his early days on the South Australian Railway give a fine insight into the atmosphere and environment of heavy hauled freight predominant on the Australian railway. His recollection of methods of training and working as a Junior Trainee Engineman will be understood by all Train Drivers and of interest to students of rail operation. Leaving Australia as a young man was obviously traumatic, but Roger's ambition to become a Train Driver never diminished. We read of a seconded experience learning new methods of working when successful in gaining employment with British Rail at Stratford, known to be the largest depot in Europe at that time.

Roger has been brave enough to admit that passing the Driver's rules examination was not easy for him. His experience of rules examination, traction training and training trips are well described. He moves through his book to give a graphic description of life as a Driver at Stratford and Bishop's Stortford, with the different forms of traction involved. Roger's view regarding the changes in working practices with the introduction of one man operation were shared by many who experienced those changes; changes that were made to facilitate the privatisation of British Rail.

My work with the National Railway Museum at York, recording the Oral History of Railwaymen, has delivered numerous accounts of life's experiences on the railway. This book is a fine addition to that history.

Lew Adams OBE
Ex General
Secretary
ASLEF

This book has been a long time coming....

a bit like some of the trains I am about to mention!

A typical South Australian country station setting, surrounded by large eucalyptus trees, in the days when the broad gauge reigned supreme. The location is Virginia, just 20¾ miles north of Adelaide on the main Port Pirie line. With the introduction of the standard gauge, this scene has gone forever.

PREFACE AND ACKNOWLEDGEMENTS

Once upon a time, in the days when steam locomotives roamed the rails of the world, it was every schoolboy's dream to become an engine driver. At any major railway terminal around the world, a group of people could always be seen admiring the locomotive at the front end. To see the person in charge of an almost living, breathing locomotive certainly inspired many a boy to follow this noble profession. In modern times, the inspiration in an electrically propelled machine just doesn't seem the same, especially when the locomotive (or traction unit to give it its clinical name) is more often at the back of the train, pushing instead of pulling. The job of driving a train is just as skilful as it has always been, especially with speeds in the region of 140 miles per hour! It seems strange, therefore, that the enthusiasm to become a train driver is no longer with us.

It was in February 1969, after the diesels had just taken over from steam traction, and I had reached my 16th birthday, that I became a Trainee Engineman for the South Australian Railways - realising a lifetime ambition. There were still a few steam locomotives working on the system, and because of this, I had to undergo training on how to fire a steam locomotive, though I have yet, to this day, to put theory into practice. In August 1970, my family returned to England, thereby giving me the chance to join British Rail at Stratford in East London. I eventually became a driver there in 1976.

Some of the photographs included in this work are not technically perfect, but have been added for their historical value. I ask for the reader's indulgence for any imperfections.

I wish to acknowledge the former **South Australian Railways** for imparting technical information while training me as an Engineman, and also the **Australian National Railways** for supplying further information. Recognition must also be given to the training from **British Rail** for placing me in my current position as a train driver. I also would like to acknowledge the photographic help of the following:-

South Australian State Transport Authority (Rail Division)

Australian Railway Historical Society (S.A. Division)

Brian Bandt of Paralowie, South Australia

Callan Davies of Blackwood, South Australia

Michael Swain of Audley End, Essex

and

Mike Rea of Elsenham, Essex.

This book is the personal account of the author's working life and the views he expresses should not be construed as those of the Associated Society of Locomotive Engineers & Firemen, Network Rail, 'One' West Anglian Railways or National Express East Anglia.

© Roger Taylor, 2009

Your Employment

with

The
South Australian Railways

The handbook that was issued to all new entrants before beginning their employment with the South Australian Railways. It spelled out the employees responsibilities regarding safety.

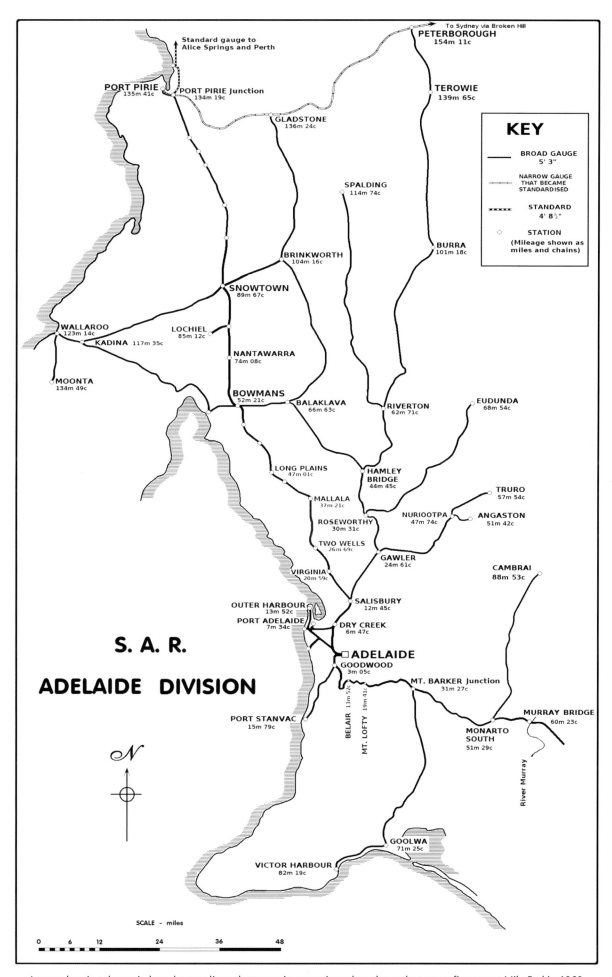

A map showing the main broad gauge lines that were in operation when the author was a fireman at Mile End in 1969.

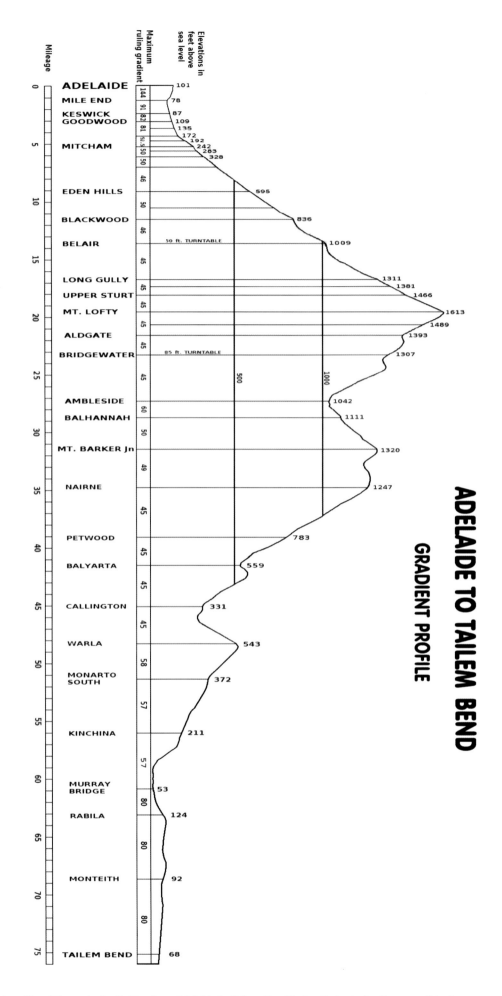

Gradient profile of the main South Line from Adelaide to Tailem Bend in South Australia. Compare this diagram with the British one on the next page for the same 75 mile distance.

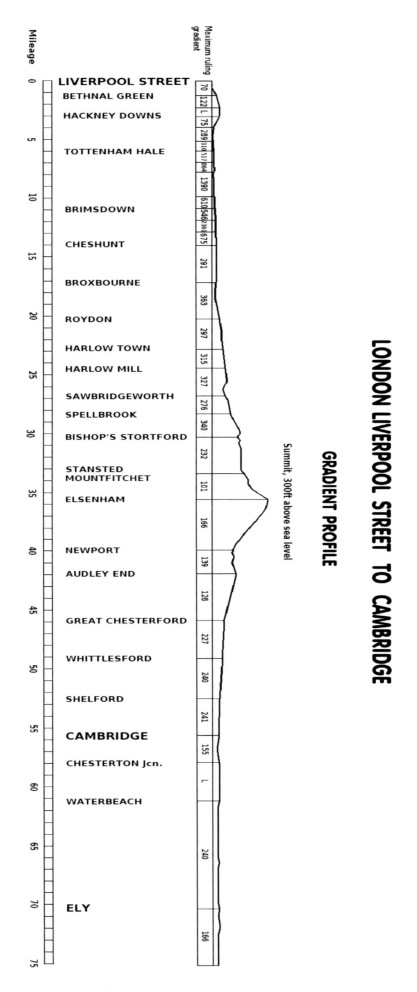

Gradient profile of the main line between London Liverpool Street and Ely. The maximum height above sea level just reaches 300' at Elsenham.

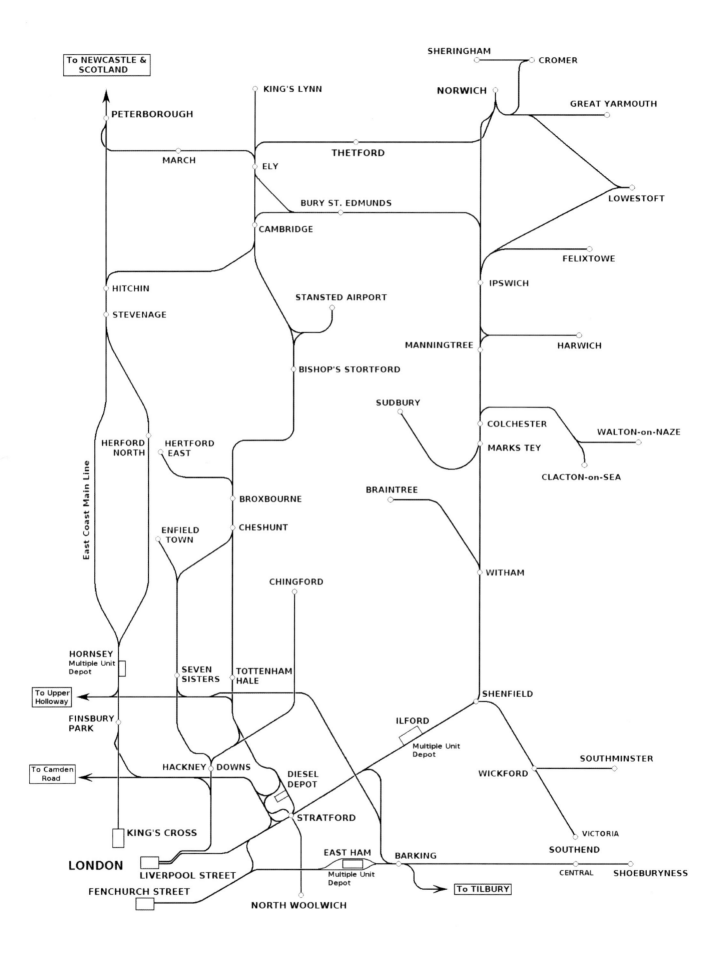

A diagrammatic map that the author drew while making route maps for drivers, showing part of the Eastern Region of British Rail that would eventually change managerial operators many times, and, at the time of writing, became owned by the National Express bus company, being known as National Express East Anglia. (National Express East Coast is from King's Cross).

INTRODUCTION

The location is somewhere in the Adelaide Hills, South Australia. The time is 15:45 on hot, dry, weekday afternoon; a period in time placed towards the end of the 1960s. The air is still, heavy with the fragrant scent of eucalyptus, laced here and there with the tangy hint of pine. Twin railway tracks lay baking in the afternoon heat, producing a shimmering heat haze in the distance. Although the air is motionless, nature envelops the listener with a variety of sounds. High in the shady gum trees the unusual warble of a piping shrike (magpie) tumbles into the afternoon stillness. A fly darts by with an unexpected buzz that fades into the distance. A few Monarch butterflies flicker their orange wings busily from bush to bush. The lilting sound of laughing and shouting children in the distance signifies that school is out for the afternoon.

This tranquillity is slowly but surely overtaken by something that, at first, resembles the hum of a busy road, but quickly increases in volume to a low growl. It soon becomes apparent that this intrusion of peace is on the move and is approaching steadily. As the intensity of the growl increases, a glance down the railway line shows that a bright headlight is appearing around the curve through the quivering haze as if by magic. The source of the ever-increasing noise then becomes blatantly obvious; interstate freight is on the move - albeit at a snail's pace. The reason for the slow speed is the fact that a thousand tons of train is climbing a gradient of 1 in 45 and has another eight-and-a-half tortuous miles to go before reaching the summit at Mount Lofty, 1,613 feet above sea level. A long blast is given on the dual-tone air horns to warn car traffic of the impending approach - as if a warning was necessary - and the melodious sound reverberates around the surrounding valley.

The din is now reaching its peak as the two maroon and silver coloured diesels blast into view. They pass in a double-screaming crescendo, both units roaring a rushing heat-haze into the azure sky at full throttle as they struggle past at a steady twenty miles per hour. The driver can be seen leaning his left arm nonchalantly on the padded armrest by the open side window. A misty oil haze is dragged along underneath the locomotives, emanating from the sump breathers.

The surroundings are now filled to choking point with diesel fumes, and the seemingly endless stream of colourful wagons dutifully trundle by following their leader. The fumes are eventually dispersed by this movement and all we are left with is the rumble of steel against steel, as the passing bogie wheels drum their rhythm against the joints in the polished rails. Well over two minutes later the familiar maroon colour of the guard's brakevan rolls by, signing off with a final 'clack-clack' as its rear bogie passes over a well-worn rail joint. The two tail lamps flicker their red lights as they disappear into a cutting and once more peace prevails, punctuated by the lingering taint of kerosene.

It was countless after-school scenes such as this that finally made me determined to become a train driver (or engineman, as they were known). The thought of sitting there like those enginemen, seeming to have no cares in the world while in control of all that horsepower, with thousands of tons in tow, certainly inspired me; trains that actually went somewhere hundreds of miles away - Melbourne, Sydney, Perth and so on. Yes, that was the life for me!

© Roger Taylor, 2009

A hot dusty afternoon sees 930-class Goodwin-Alco number 957 hauling a Tailem Bend bound freight train through Belair in the Adelaide Hills with the help of a single-cabbed sister, whilst an 830-class 'hood' locomotive is being towed along for the ride to facilitate a change-over at Tailem Bend. Numerous scenes such as this inspired me to become a train driver.

CHAPTER I
2B or not 2B?

My school reports for the end of the 1967 academic year were favourable. "Co-operative and steady worker with quite satisfactory results, although we would like to see him approach his studies with greater enthusiasm." Oh, I was enthusiastic all right, but not regarding schoolwork - especially homework. The trouble was, the Adelaide to Melbourne main line was less than half a mile away from the school and I could often be found craning my neck to look out of the window at the sound of a passing train.

"Yes Roger, it's a train. Now get on with your work." I shall always remember rushing down to the railway line after school had finished so that I could catch a glimpse of train number 669, the 15:10 goods train from Mile End to Tailem Bend. It was scheduled to pass through Coromandel station (the nearest to my high school) at about 15:45 and was always guaranteed to be a long train. The daily parade of this train roaring along at a crawl of twenty miles per hour on the steep grades towards Mount Lofty certainly helped me make my mind up about becoming a train driver.

When I first started Blackwood High School in 1966, the results of the first term looked promising; three As, three Bs and one C. As the year progressed, it was noted that I had ability in Art, as well as Mathematics. I also loved the maps associated with Geography, and my parents envisioned their son finding a niche in life as an architect or cartographer. However, the railway bug had, by then, bitten me and I certainly enjoyed the fourteen-mile round trip to school every day - by train, what else? With just a distant relative with a remote contact with railways as a guard once upon a time, it is difficult to see where the interest came from.

My very first sightings were to be of steam trains in Epping, Essex, where I was introduced to the world on a biting cold day on 23rd February in 1953. Over the next few years, I recall standing on the overhead road bridge at Epping station intently watching the approach of large chuffs of white steamy smoke as they billowed skyward. As the hissing monster 'woofed' under the bridge, I would run away, terrified, with my Dad shouting, "What's the matter? It's only a steam engine!" I was to learn later in life that these locomotives were known as F5s, not that this means a lot to me even today, other than they were 2-4-2 tank engines.

In the February of 1959, our family was to embark upon the longest one-way journey of our lives, sailing to Australia on the P&O ship *SS Strathnaver* from the Tilbury Docks, in London.

In the rural setting of Blackwood, a single 400-class diesel hydraulic railcar pauses to unload a few parcels whilst working a Saturday afternoon service to Belair with unit 402. Note the manual train destination indicator hanging from the station canopy. Note also the signal cabin, which was only opened when freight shunting was required in the yard. Blackwood was where I spent three years at high school.

I was lucky enough to be able to celebrate my sixth birthday on board as we sailed through the Mediterranean, and we crossed the equator on the 8th March 1959. Towards the end of March, we arrived at Melbourne in Victoria and we then set out on what I would call a 'decent' train journey, from Melbourne to Adelaide, on the Overland Express. The only down side about this was the fact that my three-year-old brother had the misfortune of suffering with measles during the twelve hour overnight journey. On our arrival in Adelaide, we were housed temporarily in the migrant hostel at Pennington, the grounds of which backed onto the suburban Finsbury branch line. From then on, wherever we moved we were never far away from a railway line, even though we were to move a total of nine times in about twelve years!

While we were living in a suburb called Prospect in the early 1960s, my primary school class arranged a visit to the local railway workshops at Islington, which was literally just down the road less than a mile away. I was like a dog with two tails! The visit to the workshops confirmed my interest in trains and I later visited the main offices in Adelaide Station to buy a handbook to enable me to identify various locomotives and rolling stock. It was then that I was able to distinguish between the long nosed 900-class locomotive that had an English Electric engine, and the shorter nosed 930-class that was equipped with an American Alco diesel engine, though both of these locomotives had a maroon and silver livery. I also learned that the suburban railcars were commonly known as 'Red Hens' due to their reddish-brown colour scheme (officially called Regal Red), whereas the outer suburban or long distance railcars were called 'Blue Birds'. These cars were blue and silver in colour and were each named after an Australian bird, the name written in yellow cursive lettering mid-way along the coach above the windows. A list of these names can be found at the end of this chapter.

In 1966, our family moved house to a location in the Adelaide Hills, and it was here that I started high school in Blackwood, a town a couple of miles down the road. New entrants to Blackwood High were given aptitude tests to determine which class a new pupil would be allocated to. These were classified as either A, B, C, D, or E. A and B classes dealt mainly with History and Languages, such as Latin and French, whereas C and D classes concentrated more on Art and Woodwork. The E classification was for pupils who needed extra support in their work. In my first year, I was given the choice of either 1B or 1C, so I chose 1C for the Woodwork and Art, not really wanting to learn French (a big mistake, as I was to learn later in life).

By the end of my first year at this school, we moved house once again, this time to a suburb called Goodwood. Not wanting to change schools during such an important time in my education, I stayed on at Blackwood, commuting by train for the final two years. During this time, I learned quite a lot about the railway workings along this main south line. During some of the summer months, when my parents couldn't afford to renew my season ticket, I used to cycle to and from school, but mostly I travelled the fourteen-mile round trip on 300 or 400-class diesel-hydraulic railcars. The internal layout of these trains had the driver placed in the usual left-hand-drive position within his own cubicle, which enabled passengers to be seated on the right, complete with forward facing window. Needless to say, I could always be found up there next to the driver, so after two years spent travelling this way, I knew the route like the back of my hand. In travelling up front like this, I have only ever encountered one mishap and this happened approximately halfway through my last year at school while I was on my way home to Goodwood. It had been a typical drizzly winter afternoon and we had just left Mitcham station on the way towards Adelaide. The driver had closed the throttle at about forty miles-per-hour to let the train coast to the next station. I was in my usual position perched up the front and the driver sounded the horn on the approach to Angas Road level crossing. We were just about to pass over this level crossing when I noticed something out of the corner of my right eye. Before my brain had time to register what this movement had been, there was a loud crunch and the railcar lurched about violently. We had hit a car! After we came to a screeching halt, I jumped down after the driver and offered my First Aid help that I had learned in the Boy Scouts. I eventually recounted this tale to my Mum when I reached home, and she was of the opinion that it was too dangerous to be standing at the front of the train, despite my pleas that I had not been injured in the slightest. Goodwood was the most interesting address, from a railway point of view, as it was a railway junction on the main South Line. The railway activity here was quite intensive, with suburban railcars to and from Bridgewater and Marino; outer-suburban railcars to and from Victor Harbour, Tailem Bend and Mount Gambier; local freight trains from the oil refinery at Port Stanvac and the car manufacturing plant at Tonsley; the long interstate freights to and from Melbourne and, last but not least, the hauled passenger trains to and from Tailem Bend, Mount Gambier and Melbourne. All this, as well as the occasional steam-hauled specials!

'Before my brain had time to register what this movement had been, there was a loud crunch and the railcar lurched about violently. We had hit a car!'

As mentioned earlier in the chapter, I did reasonably well in the first year at high school, so I was again given the choice of either entering classes 2B or 2C for my second year, and it became the standing joke; "2B or not 2B? That is the question." I chose 2C, and while I excelled in Art, my other subjects started to fall by the wayside. Graduating to 3C without any choice in the third year, my thoughts were still railway-minded, so I approached the South Australian Railways in their Adelaide offices, enquiring about the possibilities of becoming a train driver.

At the main enquiry desk, a large circular affair right in the centre of the cavernous railway building, my question raised a chuckle. However, I was directed to the appropriate office. Again, the question "How does one go about becoming a train driver?" seemed a comical one, often with the rejoinder "No chance," but once it was realised that I was serious, I was sat down and given the information that I required. It was pointed out that the job involved a lot of shift work, with the majority of work being performed at night. There was also a requirement to work away from home for up to three days in a row sometimes. I was relieved to find that no formal qualifications were required, other than to be able to read and write and to be fit and healthy with perfect hearing and vision. A new entrant also had to be at least sixteen years of age, which, at this stage, gave me at least ten more months to go. I was allowed to sit a preliminary aptitude test and then it was a case of wait and see.

A few months later, I received a letter from the South Australian Railways stating that I would be able to fill a vacancy for a Junior Trainee Engineman once I had reached sixteen years of age: they said that they would contact me about a week before my birthday. To my friends at school, the impending job with the railways came as no surprise.

My academic year came to its conclusion approximately a week before the Christmas of 1968, and I had visions of putting my feet up and having an easy life until my birthday came round in February. Needless to say, my mother had other ideas! I had to search the 'Jobs Vacant' pages to seek work until my career was officially under way. Personally, I think this was a bit much, considering that I was still fifteen years old, but mum was having no slackers in her house. I made my first application to a local factory that needed a young lad, but it was found that my small build was not up to hoisting around hundredweight sacks, so that was a non-starter. My second application was to an Adelaide newspaper that was advertising for a messenger boy. Their offices in North Terrace just happened to overlook the expansive yards of Adelaide Station, so if I ended up with a job here, at least I could keep an eye on the trains at the same time. I could not have sounded very enthusiastic at the interview, as I did not get this job either.

Perhaps at this stage I ought to introduce the reader to the railway system that I had been hankering to work for.

Adelaide's first railway was originally built in April 1856, constructed to a gauge of 5' 3" that became known as the broad gauge. There had been many political and engineering arguments put forward regarding the width between the running rails, and the story is too deep to go into within the realms of this publication. The Irish gauge won the day at the time and was chosen by the South Australian and Victorian Governments. In 1969, South Australia was utilising 3' 6" (narrow), 4' 8½" (standard) and broad gauges in various locations throughout the State and at stations such as Port Pirie and Gladstone, all three gauges intermixed! (Never mind a driver, who would want to be a shunter at places like that?)

It may be of interest to note that the standardisation of this mess had been considered as early as 1920, but it wasn't until 1970 that this idea had been completed with the conversion of the narrow gauge line between Port Pirie and Cockburn on the South Australia and New South Wales border, and eventually Broken Hill, but that is another story.

The main broad gauge system that I knew had very strong American influences that had been introduced in the 1940s by an ex-Missouri, Kansas and Texas railwayman, Mr. W. A. Webb. He became Railway Commissioner for the S.A.R and introduced large American-style steam locomotives to an ailing railway system. An American form of speed signalling system, brought in by the Signalling Engineer Mr. Pilkington, had already been tried and tested on some lines, and this worked on the three-position upper-quadrant principal. (This will be described in full later in this book). The British system of lower quadrant semaphore signals was still retained in remote country areas and in some shunting yards.

In the 1940s, the S.A.R were utilising a proven 4-6-0 type steam locomotive as their standard workhorse. These were known as the Rx-class and were originally built by the North British Locomotive Company in 1914 to a design very similar to the Caledonian Jones Goods locomotives in Britain. Mr. Webb was responsible for the introduction of large 4-8-2 steam power that became known as the 500-class (later modified with a booster to become the 500B-class 4-8-4s) and the 700 series 2-8-2 locomotives. These engines were built by Armstrong Whitworth and Company in Newcastle-on-Tyne and were sent to Australia by ship. This relegated the small Rx-class to lighter duties such as suburban passenger work or shunting duties.

For express passenger haulage north of Adelaide, a streamlined 4-8-4 locomotive known as the 520-class was introduced, being wholly designed and built in Adelaide but heavily influenced by the Pennsylvanian T1 4-4-4-4 locomotives in the U.S.A. The 520-class became popular with crews and enthusiasts alike, though the enclosed cabs could become extremely stifling during the summer. They had shark-nosed streamlining and were sometimes described as looking like a submarine on wheels! Strange as it may seem, some of the old Rx-class out-lived their new stable mates and were still in service as late as 1969!

Mainline diesel power was introduced in 1951 with the production of the 900-class diesel-electric locomotives. During their design stage, these diesels were originally to be powered with General Motors (EMD) engines, but again, financial and political uproar ensued, so a compromise was reached. The locomotive body design was influenced by the American Locomotive Company's (ALCO) PA-1 type, while the power plant utilised was the Mk I English Electric 16SVT engine that had been trialled in the London, Midland and Scottish locomotives 10001 and 10002. Ten of the 900s were eventually assembled at Adelaide's Islington Workshops and were a credit to English Electric and the S.A.R

Triple gauge diamond crossing located in the vast yard at Port Pirie Junction. Dual broad and narrow gauge tracks are crossed by a standard gauge track that has a Commonwealth Railways 'Budd' railcar waiting on it. The coal gantry in the distance was demolished in 1969. The locomotive depot can be seen on the right.

The striking livery of the 830-class Alco hood locomotive is obvious in this picture of number 846 as she stands waiting for her next turn of duty at Mile End Diesel Depot in ex-works condition in March 1978. These locos had a 6-cylinder in-line model 251 diesel engine fitted. This particular loco was involved in a head-on collision at Mount Lofty in March 1971.

- some of the class eventually seeing over thirty-two years of service. The 900s were originally rated at 1750 horsepower, but were derated to 1680 hp due to climatic and altitude conditions, and this enabled their longevity. Their only drawback was the single cab feature, which necessitated the use of turntables or triangles for turning facilities when worked on their own.

In 1955, slightly more powerful diesel-electrics were brought into service in the shape of the 930-class. They were a mainline diesel straight out of Alco's marketing catalogue, the DL500-B World model, built under licence by A. E. Goodwin Limited in Sydney. The first six of these units were still built with only one cab, although the rest of the class gained a flat-fronted

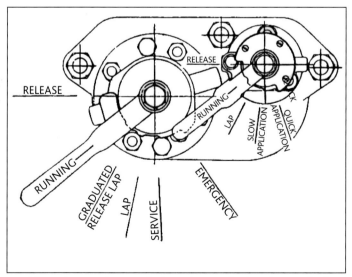

An old SAR drawing showing the basic layout of a driver's A-6-P brake valve, as used on steam locomotives. The larger handle on the left controlled the train's brakes, whilst the smaller one on the right, known as the independent brake valve, controlled just the locomotive's brakes. This layout was similar to the A-7-EL equipment that was used on diesel locomotives, except that the independent valve was on the left, and the handles were removable.
SAR / STATE TRANSPORT AUTHORITY HERITAGE COLLECTION

second cab after July 1957, when unit 936 was introduced. The bodies of these locomotives were specifically built in line with standard gauge specifications and could actually run on broad or standard gauge by changing the three-axle bogies. The 930-class were actually delivered on standard gauge bogies from the New South Wales workshops, the bogies being changed in Victoria before working onwards to Adelaide. The 900-class locomotives were built to the full broad gauge limitations, being ten feet wide at their widest point, so the bogie exchange facility was never an option for them.

A class of locomotive that was able to take full advantage of the bogie-exchange set-up was the 830-class Alco hood units. The original tender for these engines called for a lightweight locomotive, mainly intended for broad gauge branch line traffic, capable of running on standard gauge lines, but built within narrow gauge limitations - a tall order for any locomotive builder. The result from A. E. Goodwin Limited was a locomotive weighing just seventy tons, the first of which entered service on 25th February 1960. Eventually becoming general workhorses, they could be found working throughout the entire S.A.R system. A certain number of these locomotives were allocated to Tailem Bend depot specifically for working the light branch lines to places like Pinnaroo, Peebinga, Barmera and Waikerie to name a few. The 830s had a striking colour scheme of bright orange with a maroon waistband stripe that wrapped around the loco body, ending in a large diamond shape on each end. In the centre of this diamond shape was placed the South Australian state emblem, the piping shrike (magpie). The short nose on the front of these locomotives housed the Westinghouse brake equipment and the crew's toilet facilities. In later years it was preferred to run the 830s 'short end first' as the locomotives' exhaust often found its way into the cab by running 'long end first', despite having an exhaust chimney. Also, the view ahead was somewhat restricted by running this way. Loco number 844 had an experimental box arrangement around its exhaust stack to see if improvements could be made, but no other loco of this class was ever fitted this way.

Although Tailem Bend was a small town (population 1,600) seventy-five miles south-east of Adelaide, it had the railway significance of being the locomotive and crew changing point

Pacific locomotive number 628 stands at the Mile End roundhouse, clearly showing the effects of the elements and vandalism. The picture was taken in early 1968, before I joined the railways to become a Junior Trainee Engineman. This loco was eventually scrapped in August 1968.

A 620-class 'Pacific' that was lucky enough to escape the cutter's torch, newly restored 621, the *Duke Of Edinburgh*. This loco was restored in 1971 by the South Australian division of the Australian Railway Historical Society, at a cost of $10,000.
AUSTRALIAN RAILWAY HISTORICAL SOCIETY, SA DIVISION.

after trains had climbed the tortuous Mount Lofty Ranges on their way east to the State border, 121 miles away. Heavy freight trains would leave the Adelaide area (Port Adelaide, Dry Creek or Mile End) double-headed for the 19 1/2 mile, 1 in 45, climb over the hills, and once the train reached Tailem Bend anything up to four hours later, the leading locomotive would be detached, leaving the trailing loco to do the rest of the journey to the State border on its own. On reaching the border with Victoria, at a small town called Serviceton, the South Australian locos and crews would be changed with their Victorian counterparts. (It would not be until about 1980 until this ridiculous state of affairs was changed with the introduction of 'through' locomotive working.)

Many locos could be found stabled at sub depots like Port Pirie, Tailem Bend, and Mount Gambier in the Southeast, all being equipped for refuelling and light maintenance. The majority of the broad gauge fleet was allocated to Adelaide's Mile End depot, which was positioned on the western edge of the mile-long freight yards, just to the west of the city. Mile End Loco was 'home' to around 109 locomotives and it was here that the diesels would be cleaned, examined, serviced, refuelled and made ready for their next job. Major overhauls were carried out at the Islington Workshops, which were about four miles north of the city.

Hilton Road, which ran from Adelaide's West Terrace, cut across the railway yards at Mile End on an embankment, and a driveway leading to the depot ran off the northern side of this road. To the south of Hilton Road lay the old steam roundhouse, complete with an 85 foot turntable, where some steam locomotives were still kept, pending decisions on the cutter's torch. In 1968, I can remember seeing the sorry sight of a 'Pacific' (4-6-2) locomotive of the 620-class, number 628, rusting away and suffering the effects of vandalism - not a piece of glass left unbroken. I was surprised to see the locomotive's number plates still in place on the front and also on the tender sides. A recording of a 620's chime whistle, as it trails off into the distance, is still able to give me goose pimples to this day, though I have never been lucky enough to see one working in real life.

The 620-class were a light 'Pacific' built in 1936 when there became a demand for more powerful locomotives to work over branch lines. They had large smoke deflectors fitted, which gave them a decidedly French appearance. To achieve squarer valve settings, these locos had Baker valve gear fitted, but no other broad gauge loco had this due to the expense of maintenance. The locomotives worked over most of the S.A branch lines, but their main stamping ground in the end was to be the Adelaide to Tailem Bend line. Number 621 was lucky enough to be restored for main line running and was named 'Duke of Edinburgh' for its return to traffic in 1971, thanks to the hard work of the South Australian division of the Australian Railway Historical Society.

As will be noticed from all of the pictures in this book, all trains on the broad gauge were fitted with automatic couplers, usually of the Alliance bottom release type, and every traction unit, be it locomotive or railcar, was fitted with a headlight. The majority of hauled trains also had to have a guard's brakevan as the rearmost vehicle (except for trip workings between Adelaide Station and Mile End goods yard) and the reason behind this will be made clear in Chapter Three. All rolling stock on the S.A.R was fully fitted with Westinghouse Air Brake Equipment.

An air brake system required a constant supply of air, and this was provided by the compressor. These were situated on the traction unit, and supplied air for operating the brakes and the locomotive's auxiliaries such as horn, windscreen wiper and, on some locomotives, the pneumatic power controller. The main bulk of the air was stored in a cylinder called the main reservoir on the traction unit, at a maximum pressure of 100 pounds per square inch, and was fed to the rest of the train through the train pipe at a pressure of seventy pounds per square inch. Should the train pipe be accidentally parted during a journey, the loss of air would automatically apply the trains' brakes. The train pipe fed auxiliary reservoirs and a piece of equipment called a triple valve under each vehicle. The triple valve, as the name suggests, had three functions; to apply the brake, to release the brake, and to charge the train pipe (that is,

The 17:00 service to Gladstone is seen departing from Adelaide in 1969 with a 250-class Bluebird railcar towing a specially adapted refrigerated van that was painted in a matching colour scheme.

to allow the train pipe to return to seventy pounds per square inch). All this was controlled by the driver's automatic brake valve, which was one of the Westinghouse A-7-EL type on most of the mainline locomotives. Steam locos had the A-6-P type fitted, where the brake handles were not removable. Locos were also fitted with an independent brake valve that controlled just the locomotive's brakes, separate from the train brakes.

South Australia operated its trains using the single pipe method of working, which meant that just one pipe or air hose supplied air for the whole of the functions mentioned above. As one can imagine, on long trains this could take some time to perform and in some cases, mismanagement could lead to serious depletion of air. This was why most of the main line locomotives were fitted with dynamic brakes. When an electric motor is turned fast enough, it produces a current of its own and this is known as Electro-Motive Force (EMF) and dynamic braking makes use of this back EMF, through resistors, to assist in the braking of the train, but is only effective down to a speed of about fifteen miles per hour. To use the dynamic brake, the driver usually used a light application of the automatic brake to 'gather the train', then made a dynamic brake application while recharging the train pipe. Mismanagement of the correct procedure in applying the dynamic brake has resulted in spectacular derailments!

Before this chapter draws to a close, I must mention here the three types of railcar that I was familiar with during the 1960s. The depot for these units of traction was at Adelaide Station itself, and the only time Mile End enginemen had any dealings with the Adelaide men was if a Motorman was demoted to shunting duties for three months as a punishment for misconduct. As mentioned earlier in the chapter, the railcars I were very familiar with were the 300 and 400-class suburban diesel-hydraulic 'Red Hens'.

Their predecessors were the model 55 and 75 units, which were originally brought into use in the 1920s, and I can just remember their twilight years before they were scrapped altogether. They were designed by J. G. Brill in the U.S.A. and were assembled at the Islington workshops on the imported chassis. The driver virtually sat next to the engine, and to say they were boneshakers was an understatement! They were originally built with Winton petrol engines, but were later converted to diesel, mainly utilising Gardner '8L3' engines rated at 198 horsepower, although some were fitted with Cummins engines after 1959. They spent their last years in a green and cream livery with black and orange 'Day-Glo' panels on the front for extra visibility at level crossings.

Because of the increase in commuter traffic, the S.A.R introduced the 300-class single-ended diesel-hydraulic railcars in 1955. The class eventually numbered seventy-four and became colloquially known as 'Red Hens' due to their Regal Red colour scheme. Numbers 300 to 341 and 362 to 373 were powered by two General Motors 6-71 engines; the earlier batch rated at 219 horsepower, while the later units were rated at 210 horsepower.

Railcars 342 to 361 were powered by two Rolls Royce engines rated at 229 horsepower. 800-class steam-age steel coaching stock was converted, complete with guard's compartment, to become 860-class trailer cars, and the units ran as three-car sets with the trailer car in the centre. During rush hours, they could be run as six or nine-car sets. In 1959, it was realised that beyond the rush hour traffic, it was a waste of resources to run a three-car set that was virtually empty, so the 400-class power cars were introduced. These cars were similar in appearance to the 300s, except that they were provided with a driving cab at each end, with a small area set aside for the guard at one end. They were all capable of working in multiple.

Between October 1954 and November 1959, a completely new concept in railcar design revolutionised the country services on the broad gauge. Passengers travelled in air-conditioned luxury on these railcars, which were modern even by today's standards. Fully adjustable Venetian blinds were provided inside double glazed windows, and refrigerated drinking water was available free of charge. The external colour scheme of these railcars and their 100-class trailers was Royal Blue, with the body-sides under the window level featuring fluted stainless steel, which was in vogue at the time. The valance around the drawgear at each end was painted a deep yellow colour. The car numbers and corresponding bird name is given below.

POWER CARS:			
250	Quail	256	Kookaburra
251	Lowan	257	Kestrel
252	Blue Wren	258	Goshawk
253	Pelican	259	Penguin
254	Brolga	260	Corella
255	Curlew		
TRAILER CARS:			
100	Mopoke	103	Ibis
101	Grebe	104	Avocet
102	Plover	105	Snipe

LEFT: One of the bone-shaker Model 75 units sitting in the south car yard at Adelaide station in 1969. This unit, along with numbers 33 and 46, was one of the last remaining power cars left in service. Number 41 was eventually preserved by the Mile End Railway Museum in 1973.

BELOW: Diesel-hydraulic outer suburban railcar number 253 *Pelican* rests in the siding at Victor Harbour during a Saturday working in 1968. The consist is made up with a 250-class power car nearest the camera, a 100-class trailer, and a 280-class baggage car at the rear. The yellow cursive name can be seen mid-way along the car above the windows. These railcars were revolutionary for their day and are still considered modern even by today's standards.

Steam giant of the South Australian Railways; the mighty 500B-class 4-8-4 locomotive. Number 508, named *Sir Lancelot Stirling*, is seen here on the 85-foot turntable at Adelaide's Mile End roundhouse. AUSTRALIAN RAILWAY HISTORICAL SOCIETY, SA DIVISION.

The 900-class diesel-electric locomotive class leader, named *Lady Norrie*, stands at the Mile End Diesel Depot in 1969. They were powered by the famous English Electric 16SVT diesel engine, rated at 1680 horsepower. The full broad-gauge specifications can be appreciated when compared with the standard-gauge-spec 930-class Alco standing directly behind.

CHAPTER II
Hands on - almost

About the second week into February 1969, I received the letter that was to steer my life along a career path with the railways. It all seemed so matter-of-fact; I was to report to the Loco Foreman at the Mile End Diesel Depot at 08:00 on Monday 24th February, exactly one day after my sixteenth birthday. My birthday that year came and went in a blur; there was only one thing on my mind that day - Monday morning.

Eventually the inevitable happened and the morning arrived with a bright sunny start. Dad had agreed to drive me in on his way to work and I arranged to make my own way home. The depot looked impressive as the car nosed its way down the curved drive towards the office building, with diesels dotted about all over the yard simmering in the morning sun. We pulled up outside what we presumed was the Foreman's office ten minutes before eight o'clock and I took a deep breath and stepped inside the door. After introducing myself to the Foreman, he handed me a timesheet, showed me how to clock on, and told me to wait for the head cleaner. This was it; officially at work! I turned to my Dad who was waiting in the car outside, gave him a wave to let him know that I was in the right place, and bade him goodbye.

As he drove off into the distance, a thunderous roar erupted from the yard outside the office. Two of the large 900-class locomotives, coupled back to back, were being shunted by an over-zealous engineman. With the V-16 English Electric engines chugging away, the diesels moved swiftly away from the huge shed in a cloud of diesel fumes. I could see that I was going to like it here! While I waited to be introduced to the head cleaner, I meandered around the office lobby like a lost sheep, trying to make sense of some of the information in the many notice cases. By the front window was a large refrigerated soft drinks machine of the type where one lifted the lid, guided the bottle to the release mechanism, deposited the appropriate coins, then drew out the ice-cold bottle. This classic piece of American workmanship was certainly well used during the hot summers. My job for the next few months, until I qualified as a driver's mate (or fireman as they were called) was to clean the diesel locomotives inside and out. There were still a few steam locomotives roaming the system, especially on the narrow gauge, hence the name 'fireman'. Once I had passed my qualifying exams, there was a remote chance that I may get to work on one.

My daydreaming was interrupted by the entrance of a short, tubby, middle-aged man dressed in bib-and-brace overalls and a denim cap. He asked the Foreman where the 'new boy' was, and I realised that this was the man that I had been waiting for. He introduced himself as Jan Mikalac, and proceeded to show me around my prospective 'second home' and ensured that I was

900-class English Electric locomotives 905 and 908 bask in the mid-day sun outside the shed at Mile End Diesel Depot during 1969. Fellow cleaner Brian Bandt stands between the locomotives to indicate their huge size. Note that the headlights were still of the single-bulb-type. Later photographs show the locomotives with the two-bulb headlights.

allocated a locker. I never forgot his name as it was broadcast over the shed's loudspeaker system very often; usually to answer for the misdemeanours of his junior staff:-

"Jan Mikalac to the office please, Jan Mikalac to the office please!" He was of Polish descent and still retained his accent. I earned the nickname the "Leetle One" from him, as I had been the shortest, and youngest, cleaner he had ever been in charge of. There were men of various ages that were cleaners, but not all of them were in line for promotion to Engineman.

Compared to steam engines, diesels needed a very clean environment to work efficiently and the engine compartment was no exception. Air that entered the engine-room was filtered by paper filters that were soaked in oil, and these were renewed by the fitters when necessary. The general duties for the cleaner of diesel locomotives involved entering the engine-room compartment and literally wiping down the engine with rags to clean off oil seepages, then mop the floor to soak up excessive oil spillages. As one can imagine, on hot summer days, after the locomotives had struggled over the Mount Lofty Ranges, the engine-room could become blisteringly hot.

On returning home after my first day, Dad asked me what the rates of pay were and when did pay day fall. Do you know, it didn't even occur to me to ask. All I knew was that we were paid fortnightly on a Wednesday, and that they held a fortnight in hand. I was just happy to be working with the locomotives that I had been admiring all of those years, and getting paid for it just seemed incidental. My Dad's eyes rolled up to the ceiling in despair.

I found that I was one of six that were looking towards driving trains for a living, but not all were as keen as I was. If I was ever given a task, I would get stuck in straight away, whereas most of the others would drag their heels, looking forward to 'smoke-o' (tea break). It didn't take me very long to realise that, before long, I was doing the majority of the work; sometimes I was told in no uncertain terms to slow down, as I was showing up everyone else!

It was to be at least two months before we were placed on any training course, so we were meant to use our cleaning time to get to know the locomotives inside out. When cleaning jobs slackened off on some days, I would seek out some of the fitters for some technical information about the locos I was working with, just to keep out of the way. I was genuinely interested in learning, but was called a 'conshee so-and-so' (derogatory term for conscientious) by one or two of the work-shy team. Personally, I thought it was a better idea to keep out of the head cleaner's way, thereby avoiding extra chores around the depot. In this respect, I was learning fast!

As a diversion from cleaning, one or two of us would assist the depot marshaller or 'hostler' to move and position locomotives from the shed to the yard. It didn't take me long to realise that everything on the railway worked to a roster, including the locomotives. They all had to be lined up in a certain order, ready for their next turns of duty. Some of the marshallers would let us have a drive now and then, providing it was well out of sight of Mr. Moore, the Head Foreman's office. Being only five foot three, I could just about see out of the cab window, and that was with the seat raised to its full extent!

One Friday afternoon, on the 18th April 1969, the depot was abuzz with the news that a steam loco was due on shed to be prepared for an excursion the following day, organised by the South Australian division of the Australian Railway Historical Society. I asked one of my mates how he knew this was taking place, and he showed me the relevant notice in the Special Notice case in the clocking-on lobby. Sure enough, there was Train Notice number 351 from the Superintendent's office, stating that extra Guaranteed Passenger Trains would work in connection with the Aldgate Autumn Leaves Festival. Up

until that moment, I hadn't really paid these notice cases much attention, but I now realised that a lot of the time they were a source of 'inside information' about special train workings. Some were even marked "Information not to be divulged to the public." In fact, I had a ticket for this particular excursion that had been purchased via another train enthusiast at our local church fellowship club about a month previously. Never for one moment had I realised that the loco would be brought to Mile End for attention, as all preserved steam power was kept at the Islington Workshops for security reasons. About 14:30 that particular Friday afternoon, two locomotives arrived in the form of 520-class number 526, named *Duchess of Gloucester*, and Rx-class number 207, being towed by a diesel locomotive.

They were parked next to the boiler house outside the main shed in readiness for lighting up, which took about two hours on the smaller loco, but anything up to six hours on the larger locos. In the meantime, it was our job to tidy up their external appearance by using tallow wax and oil to give the locos a shiny black look. Needless to say, a couple of us stayed well beyond our clocking off time because we were so wrapped up with our special visitors. When I eventually arrived home, well over two hours later than usual, my Dad went bananas! He tried to point out that I probably wasn't going to get paid for the extra hours and that I wasn't insured to be on the premises should an accident occur. As an enthusiast, these things were the last things on my mind; I was just glad to be associated with the special occasion. On the Saturday morning, I arose early and joined the excursion from Adelaide. A good time was had by all, despite the typically drizzly autumn weather.

As is usual when young people get together at work, especially with newcomers, there were some pranks played now and then. I managed to escape the usual ones like "Can you fetch some red and yellow striped paint?" or "Go to the stores for some red oil for the red tail lamps," or even "Fetch us a bucket of steam from the stores, will you?" But I really was caught out one day whilst enquiring about the workings of the circular, concrete, windowless telephone cabinets that were used for transmitting messages between train crews and signalmen or Train Control. I was asking about the special notepads, called Train Orders, which were kept in these cabins to record certain train movements. There happened to be one of these 'phone cabins at the outlet from the depot, about half a mile from the shed. We were passing by it one day during our lunch break, when someone said "Here Roger, look at this," and, like an idiot, I went inside to see what they were on about, only to find the door slammed and locked behind me. Everything went dark and I thought that they would eventually re-open the door, but this was not the case.

I started to panic a bit, as I would be late for clocking back on for my afternoon shift, until I realised that all I needed to do was use the telephone! The trouble was, most places that this particular 'phone reached needed special coded rings on a plunger before anyone would answer. Needless to say, the Head Cleaner found me eventually. I could almost hear those immortal words again; "Jan Mikalac, to the office please...."

In May 1969, I was given a place on a training course with the Railways Institute at Adelaide, to be trained in the following subjects:-
• Cleaner's Train Working and Protection Rules
• Three Position and Automatic Block Signals
• Electric Staff and Permissive Block Working
• Train Order Working and eventually the all-important Fireman's Mechanical Course and Examination.

There came two shocks with this information, both of which I ought to have been aware of. The first came when we were informed that the course would involve a lot of homework (!)

I was just happy to be working with the locomotives that I had been admiring all of those years, and getting paid for it just seemed incidental.

without which we would not survive the course. To think that homework was the very thing that had dropped by the wayside when I was at school. The second shock came later on after we had been taught the basics of railway safety. The main chunk of our traction training would be focussed on steam locomotives, and if we did not pass this stage, the entire course would be terminated from that point on. Even as Firemen, we were supposed to know almost as much as the Enginemen regarding locomotives, to the point of being taught how to change the flexible air hoses between locos or wagons should a brake pipe or air reservoir pipe burst during a journey. Each locomotive carried a sealed toolbox for this very purpose, containing a spare Main Reservoir and Train Pipe hose and the associated spanners. Don't forget, some of the places these trains travelled to were quite remote, therefore, assistance could take some time to arrive by road.

You may recall that I mentioned earlier that there were some steam locos still around, but most of these, apart from the excursion locos, were small 4-6-0s in shunting yards. Mile End had no steam shunting locos in operation, but other places miles away still did, so it was considered essential that we learned how to fire them. The narrow gauge system further north were still using their T-class 2-8-0 and 400-class 4-8-2+2-8-4 Garratt locomotives and was still part of the S.A.R in general. We tried to object, stating that as we were working with diesels, we didn't think it was necessary to learn 'steam', but it was pointed out that our contract of employment stated that we were under obligation to accept at least one temporary transfer away from our home depot while under the employment of the South Australian Railways, which technically meant that we could be sent to a place that still had steam in operation.

This was more likely to happen to single men than married ones, but this was not a hard and fast rule. In fact the S.A.R provided married quarters for transfers if required, but the main accommodation was provided in basic barracks. Perhaps this ought to be listed as shock number three, but we took this for granted in 1969. Besides, good money could be earned while posted away to another depot so most men jumped at the chance, especially during the grain harvesting season, when extra freight trains would be run.

Eventually the time came for the six of us to attend our training classes. These were held in the Railways Institute buildings adjacent to Adelaide railway station, beside the River Torrens. The instructor chain-smoked, and, as a non-smoker, this became quite uncomfortable for me. I always looked forward to lunch breaks! It was in these backroom sessions that I learned the basics of railway safety, being drummed into us day after day. We learned how to assist the driver to protect the train in the event of a breakdown or accident, and such simple things like always facing oncoming traffic when it became necessary to walk along railway tracks. We were also taught general safety regarding the running of trains, be it on the main line or in shunting yards, like never leaving locomotives or wagons standing foul of any other line. We even had to know about all the parts of points, crossings, and junction layouts, distinguishing the difference between double slips and single turnouts. In Australia, as in America, points were commonly known as switches, because they switch trains from one track to another.

Various hand and whistle signals associated with shunting were explained, along with the recognition of various trackside appliances such as Telephone Cabinets, Switch Stands, and Outlying Switch Locks. Switch Locks were devices used to electrically lock switches (points) that were remote from a controlling signal cabin, especially in areas where there was only a local track circuit. It was essentially a timer switch housed within a locked cabinet at the trackside. When an actuating handle within the cabinet was operated by a guard or fireman, it unlocked

Streamlined 520-class locomotive, *Duchess Of Gloucester*, stands at Mile End Diesel Depot while the cleaners take a well-earned rest from preparing her for the Hamley Bridge excursion, on 1st November 1969. The roundhouse coaling tower can just be seen in the distance to the right of the picture.

the associated point rodding after sixty seconds and allowed the points to be moved. A lot of this information, boring as it may seem, was essential for firemen to know, as in some locations they had to operate the switches to let their trains into passing loops on single lines. Bear in mind that about twelve miles outside the Adelaide metropolitan area, most of the railways were, and still are, single lines. As the training progressed, we learned about lower quadrant and upper quadrant fixed signals and various methods of train working, such as Automatic Block electric signalling, Train Order Working, Electric Staff, and Permissive Block Working.

The early forms of signalling utilised in South Australia were lower quadrants, and lots of these survived into the 1980s, albeit in remote country areas and some shunting yards. The semaphore arm operated in the traditional British manner; horizontal for stop, and lowered 45° to give a proceed aspect. There were two types of lower quadrant - stop signals which were known as 'absolutes', (as in absolute block, i.e., one train in any one section or block at any one time), and distant signals. The absolutes came with either a long arm for normal operations, or a short arm where shunting was required. The short arm displayed a yellow light at night for its proceed aspect, and this allowed a train to proceed at low speed (defined as a speed not exceeding ten miles per hour). The long-armed signals were usually placed at the entrance and exit to a station yard and were known respectively as Absolute Home (which protected the yard) and Absolute Starting (which protected the section ahead) when positioned like this.

Unlike the British practice, (post 1920), the distant signal had a red painted arm with a white chevron. When the arm was horizontal, drivers were instructed to stop at the signal, then proceed at low speed towards the corresponding home signal usually from six hundred to a thousand yards away. The only time the driver was not required to stop at these signals was if the approach to the signal was on a rising gradient. The driver was then permitted to pass the red signal at low speed

An Rx-class 4-6-0 steam locomotive, number 207, pauses at Blackwood to take on water whilst working the afternoon Aldgate Autumn Leaves excursion in 1969. Locomotives such as these were still being used in some shunting yards when I first joined the railways as a cleaner.

without stopping, in case he should experience difficulty in re-starting his train on the gradient. These particular signals were recognised by the placing of a large letter 'G' (black on a white background) to the mast of the signal, and were known as Grade Distants accordingly. At night, all of these signals displayed a red light for stop and a green light for proceed.

Another difference from British practice that was rather alarming, was that at a station fully equipped with lower quadrants, the distant could show a proceed aspect with its corresponding starting signal still showing red, but only if the train was booked to stop!

Some of the remote country stations never had any fixed signals at all and if the station was attended, trains were admitted into the station by means of hand-signals. An attended station was defined as a station at which an officer or employee was on duty for train working purposes, usually a signalman or station master. Technically speaking, an unattended station would become an attended one as soon as a train arrived, as the crews were qualified to admit another train by hand-signal. When trains were sent from one station to another, they were only permitted to travel as far as the home signal of the next station or the facing points where there were no fixed signals. Before a train was permitted to enter the yard of an attended station, the driver must have received an admission signal, either by fixed signal indication or hand-signal.

At a station not equipped with any fixed signals, an admission hand-signal was given from the first facing points of the yard and was usually a green flag held steadily at arm's length by day, and a green light waved slowly from side to side at night. These hand-signals would be used whether the train was stopping or running through the station, but if the train was booked to run through but be required to stop, a red hand-signal was displayed at the first facing points. Once the train had come to a stand and the driver verbally informed of what was required, it was admitted with the green hand-signal and was not to exceed ten miles per hour, being prepared to stop if hand-signalled to do so. The train was then permitted to proceed normally. At the stations where there were no fixed signals, yard limits (normally indicated by the home and starting signal) were defined by specially erected signs stating YARD LIMIT at each end of the yard on a cast-iron oval plate measuring approximately two feet across. These indicated the limits where station shunting could be carried out. (See diagram on p14).

Automatic Block Signalling was introduced to South Australia in 1915 by the then Assistant Engineer for Yards and Signals, Mr. C.G. Pilkington, and the installation at Adelaide became

The drawing above shows an example of a lower quadrant distant signal as used by the South Australian Railways. These signals were placed approximately a thousand yards from the home signal to which they applied. Drivers were instructed to stop on sight at these signals, then proceed cautiously towards the home signal.

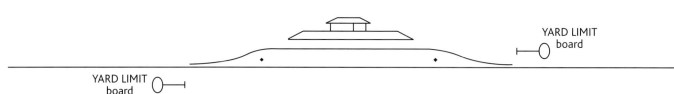

AN ATTENDED STATION
not equipped with fixed signals

YARD LIMIT board

YARD LIMIT board

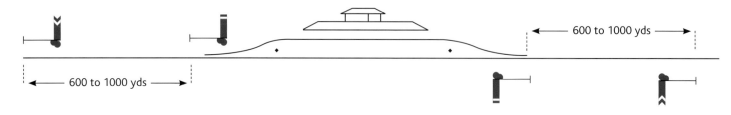

AN ATTENDED STATION
equipped with Absolute 'Home' signals

600 to 1000 yds

600 to 1000 yds

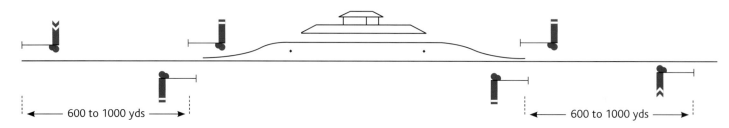

AN ATTENDED STATION
fully equipped with lower quadrant signals

600 to 1000 yds

600 to 1000 yds

The above drawings indicate what the layout of stations in lower quadrant territory looked like.

the first major terminal in the Southern Hemisphere to be fully equipped with electric three-position upper-quadrant signalling, complete with point motors and electric interlocking. This system of signalling, sometimes known as Speed Signalling, assumed that a driver did not need to know the route over which he was about to travel but just the speed. The three speeds involved with this type of working were as follows:-

• Normal Speed - The speed set down in the Working Time Table for a particular length of line.

• Medium Speed - The speed set down in the W.T.T. for a particular length of line, which did not exceed twenty miles per hour.

• Low Speed - A speed which would enable the driver to stop his train within half the distance if the line ahead was seen to be clear, and which did not exceed ten miles per hour.

The Automatic Block signals that were eventually employed extensively by the S.A.R. were divided into two categories - semaphores and colour-lights. Each arm on a semaphore indicated the speed at which the train was permitted to travel through the section ahead. When the top arm operated, the train was allowed to travel at normal speed. When the second or middle arm operated, the train must travel at medium speed, usually because the train was being diverted from the straight route at a set of points.

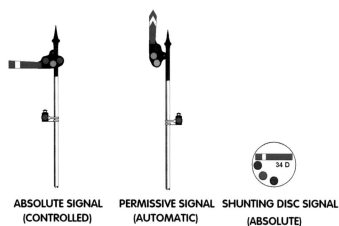

ABSOLUTE SIGNAL (CONTROLLED)   **PERMISSIVE SIGNAL (AUTOMATIC)**   **SHUNTING DISC SIGNAL (ABSOLUTE)**

The signal on the left is an example of a single-armed three-position upper quadrant absolute, showing the vertical alignment between the main red aspect and the marker light. The signal in the centre is a three-position permissive, and the alignment between the main green aspect and the marker light is staggered. On the right, not to the same scale, is a three-position disc shunting signal showing the purple lens used for the stop indication.

For a stop indication, the arm was horizontal and showed a red light at night. When the arm was raised to an angle of 45° with a yellow light at night, this indicated to the driver that the next signal was showing a stop indication, and was known as a caution aspect. If the section ahead was clear, the arm was raised to 90° showing a green light at night, and this told the driver that he could travel at normal speed. If the train was to be diverted from the straight route at a set of points, a second arm was added to the mast below the main arm. The lower arm always indicated medium speed, which was defined as a speed not exceeding 20 miles per hour. At certain locations, shunting was sometimes required and in this case, a shorter third arm could be found on the signal post. This arm could only be raised to 45° and showed a yellow light at night, indicating to the driver that the movement was not to exceed ten miles per hour. Stations such as Adelaide utilised disc shunting signals, and also used them as platform starting signals.

Sometimes these discs used a purple light for the stop indication on the main line so that drivers weren't confronted with a red light unexpectedly.

The colour of the arms on these signals was red with a white stripe, similar to the lower quadrants. Controlled signals had the square-ended arm and were also known as absolutes. The automatic signals had a pointed arm, the reverse of a fishtail, and were known as permissives. To differentiate between these types at night, the lights on an absolute read in a vertical alignment, whereas the permissives read in a staggered alignment. On a signal with only one arm, a marker light was added to the post below the arm.

Colour-light signals operated on exactly the same principle, but gave their indications with lights both day and night with either single-lens searchlight types or three-aspect groups.

The signals located at a station with a signal cabin were electrically controlled by the signalman from the stop to the caution position only, the rest being automatically controlled by the next signal in advance through a low voltage track circuit system. The passage of a train automatically returned the signal to the stop position. Railwaymen used the term 'stick' in place of 'signal' because controlled signals would stick at the Stop indication until the signalman either re-set the signal, or switched over to automatic operating. When the cabin was closed, the indication was governed by the next signal in advance. The map on page 16 shows the general layout of an unattended station on Automatic Signal Territory.

When a driver approached an absolute signal showing a stop

indication, he would first of all give a code whistle on the horn (a series of long and / or short blasts that varied from station to station) to challenge the signal's indication. If, after bringing the train to a stand, it was found that the signal could not be operated due to defect or other reason, the driver had to wait for written authority before the signal was passed. At an attended station with a signal cabin, the signalman issued the driver with a Caution Order slip (form 142). The order would have stated that the signal(s) concerned could be passed at danger at low speed up to the next signal, or through station limits if there was no signal in advance. Trains had to travel at low speed in case the signal was being held at danger by the effect of a broken rail.

A different method was used to give written authority to pass a signal at danger when the following situations applied:-
• Should the affected signal be at an unattended station or the controlling signal cabin be closed,
• When the signal was at a distance from the controlling signal cabin and an undue delay would occur in obtaining a Caution Order,
• If the signal was at the entrance to Electric Staff or Train Order territory,
• or when the signal was at the entrance to a tunnel.

In these cases, the driver had to obtain a Train Order (form 377) which were issued and dictated by the Train Controller over the telephone. These will be described in more detail later in the book.

When a train was brought to a stand at a permissive signal showing a Stop indication, if it didn't clear within one minute, basic ruling permitted the driver to pass the signal at danger at low speed; hence the name 'permissive'. This was known as the 'one minute rule' covered by Rule 107(c) in the Rule Book. Victoria ran a 'ten second' rule on their system! If the driver saw a train ahead that had stopped, the following train also had to stop no nearer than one hundred yards from the rear of the train in front, and was only allowed to draw closer if hand-signalled to do so by the guard of the preceding train.

The mechanical side of my training was initially based on steam locomotives, and I was eventually able to trace the passage of steam from the time it left the boiler until it reached the atmosphere, via such things as the driver's regulator valve, steam chests, cylinders, slide valves and exhaust pipe. All very boring for a lad fresh out of school; all I wanted to do was get in the cab and drive a train!

When the period of training came to an end, we sat the relevant exams and were sent back to Mile End to carry on cleaning, eagerly awaiting the final results. On the 21st July

Above is an example of a Caution Order that was issued to drivers, giving them authority to pass signals at danger. This would have only been issued once any points involved had been checked and were set correctly for the move about to be made.
SAR / STATE TRANSPORT AUTHORITY HERITAGE COLLECTION.

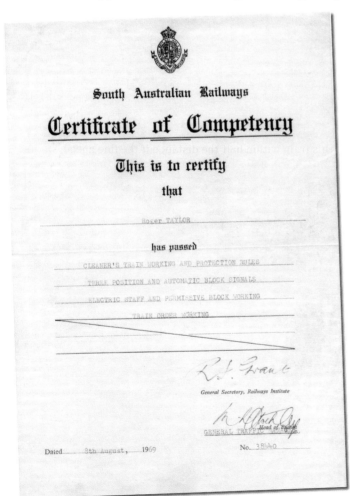

An SAR Certificate of Competency.

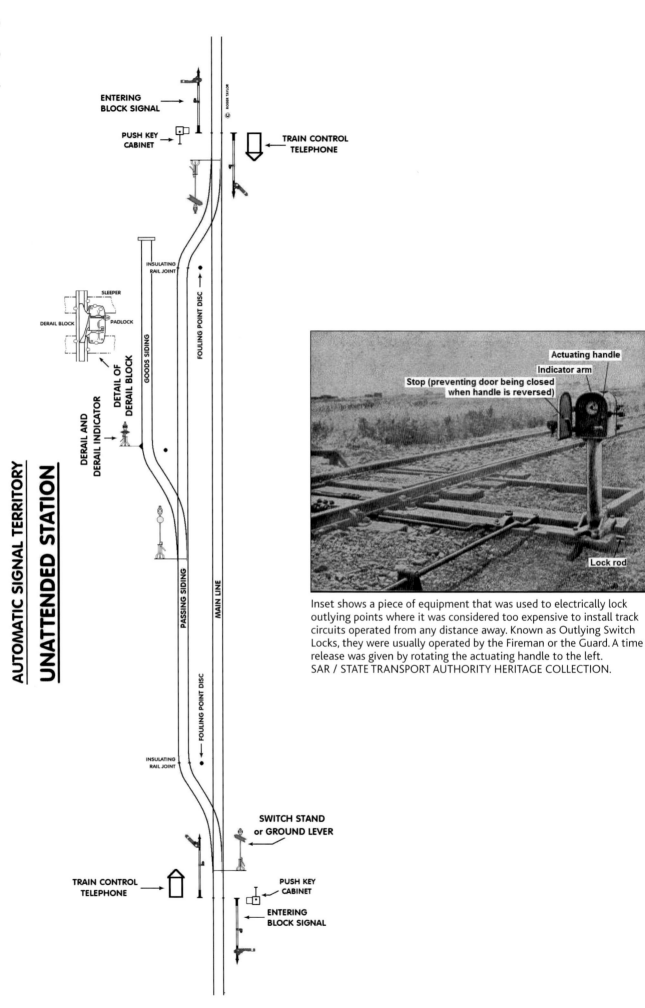

The track layout of a typical unattended station in rural areas where train crews admitted themselves into the passing siding.

S. A. R.

AUTOMATIC SIGNAL TERRITORY
UNATTENDED STATION

ENTERING BLOCK SIGNAL

PUSH KEY CABINET

© ROGER TAYLOR

TRAIN CONTROL TELEPHONE

INSULATING RAIL JOINT

FOULING POINT DISC

SLEEPER

DERAIL BLOCK

PADLOCK

DETAIL OF DERAIL BLOCK

DERAIL AND DERAIL INDICATOR

GOODS SIDING

PASSING SIDING

MAIN LINE

FOULING POINT DISC

INSULATING RAIL JOINT

SWITCH STAND or GROUND LEVER

TRAIN CONTROL TELEPHONE

PUSH KEY CABINET

ENTERING BLOCK SIGNAL

Actuating handle

Indicator arm

Stop (preventing door being closed when handle is reversed)

Lock rod

Inset shows a piece of equipment that was used to electrically lock outlying points where it was considered too expensive to install track circuits operated from any distance away. Known as Outlying Switch Locks, they were usually operated by the Fireman or the Guard. A time release was given by rotating the actuating handle to the left.
SAR / STATE TRANSPORT AUTHORITY HERITAGE COLLECTION.

1969, we were allowed an extended lunch break to watch a piece of history taking place on the television. We all packed ourselves into the canteen to hear the immortal words from a certain Neil Armstrong, "That's one small step for man, one giant leap for mankind." *Apollo 11* had landed on the moon!

On the 8th August 1969, I passed all of the relevant exams and received a certificate signed by the General Traffic Manager, Mr. Murray L. Stockley (who later became the Acting Commissioner). In September, I sat for the final cleaner's preliminary exam that would allow me to actually work on trains for real, rather than on paper. Passing this exam on the 12th September, I was greeted with a stumbling block. Because I was still only sixteen, I wasn't legally allowed to take up shift work, therefore I had to wait another five months until 23rd February, 1970. This basically meant back to the proverbial drawing board, cleaning locos at Mile End until this date came round.

It was during this lull in the proceedings that my career nearly came to an abrupt end, despite all of the safety training. The platforms and tracks within the loco shed at Mile End were placed on stilts to allow maintenance staff to gain access underneath locomotives to examine traction motors and change brake blocks. I had been in the engine room of a 930-class Alco that was coupled back-to-back with another, and, having finished the job in hand, I left the cab at the point where it was coupled to the other unit. The rear cabs of 930s were flat-fronted, and the exit door was located on the end of the loco rather than on the side. This was to allow firemen to gain access to each locomotive, to enable them to physically examine the engines on long trips. To leave the loco altogether, one had to walk along a six inch ledge while holding onto the appropriate handrail. Once the external corner of the cab was reached, one either climbed down the relevant steps or stepped straight onto a station platform. This was what I was doing on this particular day, and as the locos were coupled back-to-back, I had one foot on one loco's ledge and the other foot on the other loco.

I let go of the handrails to step onto the shed's platform and, being distracted by my mates, put my foot into thin air by mistake! I fell between the two locomotives and the raised platform, narrowly missing hitting my chin on the platform edge, and dropped ten feet to the floor below. Two of my colleagues, having noticed my sudden disappearance, instantly realised what had happened and raised the alarm. I was carried to the first-aid room where I was given a check-over, and luckily it was found that I had only bruised my hip. It was a close shave for me and it taught me a valuable lesson. Never be complacent when on or near trains!

Whilst I was still cleaning, I had some unusual experiences. Usually, when we were busy cleaning the engine room, there were other staff engaged in carrying out their duties at the same time. There would be fitters giving the diesels a technical 'once-over' and also a man employed to check the engine sump oil level. This would involve removing one of the engine's crank-case covers and, by using a large dipstick, determine whether the oil needed topping up. If this was the case, a twenty-five gallon drum of oil would be wheeled up to the side access door of the engine room and emptied directly into the sump *via* a specially constructed 'trough'. There were certain precautions to be taken on a hot engine before opening the crank-case covers, and twice I have experienced crank-case explosions when these precautions were not adhered to. On another occasion, I was busy in the engine room (again) and the fitters started to run the engine up to maximum revs to give an audible check, when there was an almighty flash and a bang due to the main generator having a flashover. I was like a rat out of a drainpipe; I've never left an engine room so fast! Apparently, a flashover is brought about by dust or dirt in the generator and causes the commutator to arc all the way round, causing a short circuit and explosion!

One of my most unusual duties that I performed while I was still a cleaner involved being a 'rider'. One day, a decision was made to haul away some of the old steam locos that had been rusting away around the Mile End roundhouse to the Islington Workshops ready for scrapping. The silent steamers had been stripped down to bare basics ready to be hauled away, and this included all the air hoses

A LIMA 'HO' scale model of a 930-class locomotive in Australian National colours demonstrates quite clearly the narrow ledge that was used for exiting the B-end cab.

and brake cylinders. As this left them technically without air brakes, someone was required to ride in the cab of each locomotive to furiously wind on the handbrake should the locomotives become uncoupled from each other during the journey. With all rolling stock on the S.A.R broad gauge system being fitted with Alliance automatic couplers, it was unlikely that an uncoupling event would take place, but riders were utilised for basic safety reasons. Only qualified personnel were allowed to act in this capacity and, as I had passed my exams by this stage, I was given the opportunity. Besides, it gave me a welcome break from the tedious cleaning duties.

An 830-class diesel was utilised to haul the rusty collection of steam locos, and off we trundled at a steady twenty miles per hour. I was seated in an old Rx-class, and even at twenty miles per hour the ride was rough! Alas, I never thought to make a note of any locomotive numbers at the time. After leaving the old locos in the confines of the scrap road at the Islington Workshop's yard, we all huddled into the cab of the 830 loco for the trip back to Mile End.

An unusual incident happened to me one day while I was catching a lift on a diesel. My cleaning shift had finished for the day and I had decided to ride into Adelaide on the loco that was assigned to work the afternoon passenger train to Tailem Bend, mainly because it was a 900-class - one of my all-time favourite types of locomotive. Because the single-cabbed loco was facing the wrong way round, (the yard marshaller obviously had not done his job properly), it needed turning on the roundhouse turntable, and this is where the trouble started. As you can imagine, the rear view was somewhat restricted when running like this, and I was assisting the crew in keeping a lookout. As we passed under the Hilton Road bridge, I noticed that a Railway Departmental road vehicle was attempting to cross the tracks behind us as we were reversing towards the turntable. The truck stopped when its driver noticed our approach. I shouted over to our driver that I thought that the truck was a bit close to our track, and his fireman leaned out to check, sounding the horn at the same time as a precautionary measure. This was followed by a sickening crunch of metal against metal as the rear skirting of the locomotive struck the bonnet of the road vehicle. The diesel was considered unfit to take into service, so it was returned to the shed for a replacement, and I then decided to catch the usual railcar to go home on. Luckily no-one was injured in the incident, but I couldn't work out why the truck driver never realised that his vehicle was standing foul of the railway track.

This picture shows the short arm of a lower quadrant signal cleared for a shunting movement controlled by the North End Scissors Cabin, with the Diesel Depot point man's hut just visible on the bottom left of the picture.

Lower quadrant shunting signals at the North Arrival yard at Mile End that were used for reversing movements.

930-class Goodwin-Alco number 952 heads a line-up of locomotives at the Mile End Diesel Depot in 1969, with me sitting in the driver's seat whilst still a cleaner. It was at this stage that I was waiting for my seventeenth birthday to arrive, to enable me to work on the main line for real.

A cab-side view of the only broad gauge diesel locomotive to receive a name, complete with tea stains, class leader number 900. This locomotive was named after the wife of the Governor General of South Australia, Sir Willoughby Norrie. Note the stable-type doors, which were a boon during the hot summers. They also allowed safe exchanges of the Electric staff by hand.

A 500-class diesel-electric shunting locomotive is seen in the northern carriage sidings at Adelaide station in 1969. I was the fireman on this loco, having started duty at six o'clock in the morning. Note the two kerosene tail lamps on the running board near the front of the locomotive.

CHAPTER III
Around the System

After passing the final written exams, we were given a trial day out under the supervision of a Locomotive Inspector, to see if we could put theory into practice. The train chosen for this 'taster' day was the 12:30 afternoon passenger service from Adelaide to Port Pirie and back, otherwise known as the East-West Express. This train was the connection for passengers travelling from Eastern states on the Overland Express, intending to travel further westwards on the standard gauge Transcontinental service operated by the Commonwealth Railways from Port Pirie to Kalgoorlie in Western Australia. This was an interesting choice for trainees, as the trip involved a lot of Electric Staff Working. It was certainly interesting for me, as this train was regularly rostered a 900-class locomotive.

The Electric Staff method of working was used on single lines, and the authority for a driver to allow his train to enter a single line section was the possession of a metal rod known as an Electric Staff. This staff, or token, was ten and three-quarter inches long, and had grooves and ridges along its length, the arrangement of these grooves differing for each section of line. The names of the stations to which the staff applied were engraved at one end of the staff, with each staff being numbered. All train movements under this form of working were under the direction of the Train Controller. This type of working was considered safe in that only one staff could be obtained from a pair of instruments at the one time. Once this was done, the pair of instruments became electrically locked, preventing more than one staff being withdrawn and thereby preventing more than one train being in a section at the same time. The penalty for a driver entering a section without the staff was instant dismissal. The term 'a pair of instruments' meant there were two instruments, one at each end of the section, and the staffs for that section only will fit into the instruments of that pair.

There were two types of staff, the metal brass-ended type, and the lightweight Duralumin type. The collection of an Electric Staff was usually carried out by the fireman, in collaboration with either the stationmaster or signalman at an attended station, or the guard of the train concerned at unattended stations. The exchanging of these staffs could be carried out 'on the move' either by hand, or by the automatic exchanger apparatus. The manual method used large cane hoops and could be exchanged at a speed of fifteen miles per hour should the train not be stopping. When exchanging staffs with the automatic apparatus, the staff was strapped to a small metal hoop and exchanged at speeds of up to fifty miles per hour. The throwing of an Electric Staff onto the ground was extremely frowned upon, as it was likely to cause damage to the grooves on the staff, possibly preventing it from being returned to its respective instrument.

The apparatus on the locomotive for exchanging the staffs automatically was operated by the fireman, and was situated on the right-hand side of the locomotive beneath the fireman's seat. On the 900-class locomotives, the catcher was placed just behind the fireman's seat and underneath the radio equipment bracket. Invariably, a novice fireman, collecting a staff this way for the first time, would strike his head upon the radio bracket in his eagerness to bring the staff into the cab. I am sure that the inspectors on the training trip, mentioned earlier, were secretly betting on how many of us would hit our heads on this bracket. I know I did! It was always said that one only ever had this happen once, hopefully learning from one's mistake. The catcher part of the apparatus was shaped like a ram's horn and was lowered to the horizontal position by a hand lever. This dropped the catcher outwards to a position that engaged the staff holder held by the ground apparatus at the trackside. It was drummed into us that care was to be exercised at stations where the passenger platform was on the same side as the exchanger, and for this reason, the ground equipment was placed about two hundred feet before reaching the platform. The trick was to raise the catcher as quickly as possible after an exchange, to prevent the catcher striking the platform edge!

As soon as the train crew was in possession of the staff, the driver and fireman must both check that they held the correct staff for the section ahead and then place it in a position near the driver so that both of the crew were able to see it. At some unattended stations, the points were provided with an Electric Staff Drawer Lock. This was basically a metal box that had a drawer with a grooved recess in it that could hold the staff for that particular section. To unlock the points, the Electric Staff must be placed into the opened drawer, which was then fully closed. This action then unlocked the points to enable them to be reversed.

Broad gauge lines that were worked under the Electric Staff Block System whilst I was employed by the SAR are:
- Salisbury to Bowmans, Snowtown and Port Pirie Junction (withdrawn 29th May 1982)
- Hamley Bridge to Riverton and Terowie
- Pooraka and Northfield (Special staff - one train only)
- Albert Park and Hendon (Special token staff working, one train only)
- Port Adelaide Cabin 'A' and Dry Creek
- North Gawler to Nuriootpa and Angaston
- Tailem Bend to Wolseley and Serviceton.

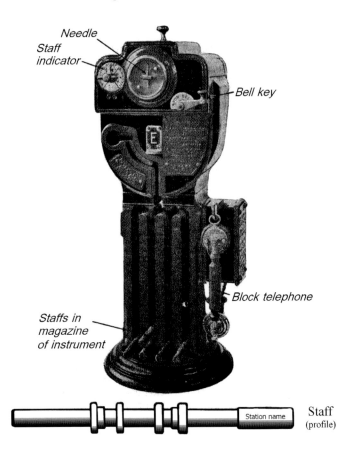

Needle
Staff indicator
Bell key
Block telephone
Staffs in magazine of instrument
Station name *Staff (profile)*

A typical SAR Electric Staff Instrument.
SAR / STATE TRANSPORT AUTHORITY HERITAGE COLLECTION

(In the mid 1980s, Centralised Traffic Control brought an end to this kind of working in South Australia.)

My career as a fireman would basically follow the same steps up the promotion ladder as that of a driver. I would be starting out as a shunt fireman and then moving on to work local goods trains in the suburban area around Adelaide. After this, I would then be promoted to roadside goods-train fireman and eventually express goods work. Once this stage was reached, I would then be promoted to passenger work, being involved with trains like the East-West, the Broken Hill Express and the prestigious Overland Express. During this stage of my career, I would then be expected to attend further training courses to prepare me for the eventual position as a driver. The whole process would then start all over again.

Eventually the day came when my seventeenth birthday allowed me to venture out onto the mainline as a fully-fledged fireman, although I was given the title of Acting Fireman until I had completed a certain number of shifts within the grade. The word 'mainline' was used rather loosely, as my first firing turns were in the shunting yards at Mile End, requiring an early start of five o'clock on the Monday morning to allow the 500-class shunt locomotives to be prepared on depot for the week's work ahead. It was part of the fireman's duties to assist the driver in starting up the engine by opening one of the side panels on the engine-room hood and priming the lubricating oil system by a hand pump. Overall, there were eight shunt locos to prepare - seven for the Mile End yard and one for Adelaide station. The number one shunter was used in the main North Arrivals part of Mile End. Number two was utilised in the North Departure sidings, while number three was situated in the New Yard, and number four sat in the South Arrival Yard awaiting trains from Tailem Bend. The South Departure sidings was the home for number five shunter, and number six busied itself with cold store trips along Railway Terrace, which ran parallel with the western edge of Mile End Yard. Number seven shunter was assigned to the East Yard where two major carriers' sheds were located. This is what made Mile End an important freight terminal, as opposed to just a large marshalling yard. The main carriers that I can remember were TNT (Thomas National Transport), Brambles, Alltrans and Mayne Nickless. These firms' containers were loaded either straight onto flat cars built for the purpose, or lifted into open gondola wagons.

The eight-hour shift was spent on the locomotive, with a short meal break when time permitted. The crews were only allowed to leave the locomotive once their respective relief crew turned up for duty. There was no going home early if shunting had finished, because the crews had to return to the depot to file any reports and clock off under the strict supervision of the Foreman, day or night. On night shifts, if time permitted during breaks in shunting, the crews sometimes managed to stretch out on the floor of the cab to get forty winks. It took a long time before my body clock ever adjusted to shift patterns, something like five years!

When wagons were shunted around in freight yards, the air that was used to operate the brakes was drained out of each vehicle to enable them to be moved around at will. This meant that one or more wagons could be shoved along, then uncoupled from the propelling locomotive to roll along by themselves. On the arrival of a lengthy Interstate freight, men were employed to pull the release cords on all of the vehicles, whilst shunters weighed up which group of wagons had to be shunted onto which track and in which order. The fireman's duties on a shunting loco were just as important as on the main line, as a good lookout was required at all times. This meant assisting the driver in looking out for a shunter's hand signal, or keeping an eye on fixed signals to the rear of the movement being made. Notice that I said 'assist' not 'interfere', and this fact was brought home to me rather abruptly one day. On this particular day, our 500-class shunting loco was having difficulty in moving a string of wagons. The driver took power, the in-line English Electric 4SRKT engine revved away, but the wagons would not budge. The shunter kept frantically waving his arms, the loco

The illustration above shows the arrangement of a switch stand that was equipped with an Electric Staff Drawer Lock. The rodding trailing towards the centre of the picture was connected to a derail block that was situated around the right-hand curve. Note that the arrow target on the switch stand does not point to the direction that the points were set. SAR / STATE TRANSPORT AUTHORITY HERITAGE COLLECTION

kept shuddering away, slowly inching the vans forward, but not a lot of progress was being made. This was because some of the brakes had not been released thoroughly and were dragging on some of the vehicles. I thought I would help by stepping on the sander button located on the floor, to assist the loco in gaining adhesion. The driver slammed the throttle shut and applied the brakes. "What are you doing?" was the question aimed at me. I sheepishly muttered that I thought I was helping by applying some sand to the rails.

His reply was short and not very sweet: "If I want your help, I'll ask for it!" As you can imagine, the atmosphere in the cab was a bit frosty for the rest of the shift.

Performing shunting duties in Adelaide station was quite interesting, as one could observe the comings and goings from this thirteen-platform terminal. On the early morning shift, one of the duties involved taking a couple of large ice blocks down to the Wye Cabin, a British-looking signal cabin located just out of the main terminal. This supplied the cabin with cool drinking water. During these early hours of the day, smells of hops and malt drifted across the yard from the Adelaide Brewing Company's premises on North Terrace, the significance of which I didn't appreciate until later in life! Shunting duties in Adelaide involved removing the coaches, in two nine-carriage portions, of the Overland Express once it had arrived from Melbourne. Before this could be done, the linen from the sleeper cars had to be removed and taken to the laundry, which was situated nearby on the northern side of the station. Once these cars had been dragged into the yard and pushed through the washing plant, and eventually stabled in their own shed, it was then time to push out the coaches for the 12:30 East-West Express for Port Pirie. The consist for this train varied according to demand.

Sometimes, jobs that were more interesting could be had when rostered for pilot duty. Normally this involved a crew standing

A freight train from Mile End to Port Pirie is about to collect the Electric Staff (circled) from the ground apparatus at Salisbury station, the starting point of Electric Staff Working on the North Line.

A close-up view of the Electric Staff catcher on the fireman's side of a 930-class Alco locomotive.

A panoramic view of the Mile End Goods Yard in 1969, taken from the coaling tower near the roundhouse. In the centre-right of the picture (arrowed), a 500-class diesel shunting locomotive can be seen tucked just inside what was known as the Inwards Goods Shed. Note the different styles of brake vans in evidence; two 8300-class, and two of the older caboose-style brake vans that had a passenger compartment at one end. The wagons in the foreground are sitting in what was the South Arrival yard. Towards the background on the right is Adelaide's West Terrace cemetery, with the City skyline situated on the left.

by to run locomotives from the depot to trains standing in Mile End Yard. If someone called in sick for a particular job, it would fall upon the pilot crew to take up the job involved. About half of the set workings were fairly local jobs, but the other half would involve working away from home for up to three days. For this reason, enough food (including tea and sugar) was to be brought with you to sustain you for the two days at least. Given the very high temperatures experienced in the summertime, milk would not keep for more than five minutes out of a refrigerator. An ingenious way around this problem was to carry condensed milk that came in a handy toothpaste-style tube. This not only provided milk for tea or coffee, but also acted as a sweetener at the same time. These supplies, along with a plastic plate and knife and fork, were commonly carried in a tin box that was slung over the shoulder, and the long jobs were colloquially known as 'box jobs'. Most of the people that I knew looked forward to these jobs, as it meant extra payments were added to the day's wage in the form of a meal allowance, a lodging allowance, long shift allowance, and a distance allowance for working over a certain mileage. There were even extra payments for working with dual or triple locomotives, as each locomotive had to be regularly examined during each trip.

More often than not, these 'box jobs' required the use of barracks once the destination was reached, due to the hours already worked. The usual practice on arrival was to locate the set of keys to a vacant room from the signing-on point, chalk one's name onto a blackboard in readiness for a return trip, then try to get some sleep. The minimum break between turns was eight hours. Getting any sleep at all was sometimes easier said than done, as the barracks were often just a stone's throw from the railway yards, as was the case at Port Pirie, where shunting was continually taking place. These barracks were pretty basic affairs, consisting of a number of bedrooms with a common kitchen and mess area. Generally, the barracks were in pretty poor repair and often over-run with mice. They were more suited to a single man, as the jobs could take one away from home for up to three consecutive days. Some men didn't complain, as it gave them the chance to get away from the 'other half' for a few days and have plenty of liquid refreshment in the local hostelries. Overall, in the long term, it did harm to some relationships and it was considered an out-dated practice. In my time as a Fireman, I sampled the delights of Port Pirie and

An English Electric 500-class shunting locomotive, number 506, is seen performing in platform eleven at Adelaide Station in 1969, with the shunter clinging on to the purpose-made steps. Judging by the time of the day, it has probably just placed the carriages in readiness for the 12:30 East-West Express to Port Pirie.

Snowtown barracks.

During one of the spells doing the afternoon pilot duty at Mile End, I fell in for firing the evening staff train from the Islington Workshops to Mitcham. On this particular day, we were given an English Electric 800-class for the job. These locomotives were equipped with an English Electric 6SRKT six-cylinder in-line engine of 800 horsepower. We hooked onto our train, usually a set of old suburban cars that looked as if they came straight out of the Wild West, and performed the test to make sure that the brakes were working properly (known as a continuity test). These end-loading cars were originally built for the Glenelg Line tramway and were built to a wider gauge than normal, being ten feet wide. We set away from Islington, approached Torrens Bridge Junction, then rounded the Gaol Loop curve. This curve allows trains to by-pass Adelaide station. After departing Mile End station, the driver asked me if I knew my way around this area. I replied that I wasn't too sure, thinking that he meant the streets in the Mile End area. What he actually meant was, did I know the railway route to Mitcham; he was offering me the chance to drive the train if I wanted. Well, having spent two

A close-up view of the train crew barracks at Snowtown. They were an arrangement of sleeping quarters with a common kitchen. Although the setting seemed tranquil amongst the eucalyptus trees, the barracks were just a stones throw from the main line. As could be expected in a large grain loading station, there were plenty of mice to keep you company!

years travelling to and from school up and down this line, I certainly knew 'the road', so my answer lost me the opportunity to have a drive. Once this train reached Mitcham, the three cars were placed in the siding next to the station yard and left there for the return trip in the morning. Our job was to then take any freight wagons that were offering back to Mile End. Mitcham yard was used for the unloading of firewood that came in the form of small tree roots. Having come from the area north-east of Tailem Bend that was known as the Mallee scrubland, these roots were commonly called Mallee roots.

Another interesting job I managed to fall in for one Saturday afternoon, whilst carrying out pilot duty, was working an Extra Goods to Tailem bend. This train, a string of loaded four-wheeled 20 ton stone wagons, was not in the normal Working Time Table and was basically a departmental working. We were given a pair of 900s for the task of climbing the Mount Lofty ranges, where the ruling gradient was a severe 1 in 45. It was after leaving Mitcham that the terrain changed to quite rugged scenery, involving numerous 10 chain radius curves, with a few tunnels thrown in for good measure. Once the weight of our train started to take hold when we hit the 1 in 45 gradients at the foot of the Adelaide Hills, the locos started to struggle. What didn't help was the light drizzle that had started to fall. The 900s started to slip and when this happened, power dropped off, and then came back with a surge.

The growling V-16 English Electric diesel engine produced some throaty exhaust sound as we slowly crawled around the curve after leaving Sleeps Hill tunnel - absolute music to my ears! The speed started to drop, and with this, the main generator's field diverts dropped out. This is a built-in feature to prevent over-heating the traction motors whilst under sustained heavy load. We eventually gained full control and rumbled through Blackwood station at about 22 miles per hour. Once we arrived at Tailem Bend, almost 2½ hours later, it was time for a quick cup of tea, then back to Mile End with a few empty wagons. The SAR rarely sent locomotives 'light engine' (loco without a train) if they could possibly help it, often coupling them onto a booked service to get them back to where they were needed.

On the 13th of April 1970, I had the misfortune of misreading my roster regarding my next turn of duty. The Railways were still using the twelve hour clock system, and I thought I had been given a particular day off, followed by a shift starting at 11:45 a.m. When I turned up for duty, the Foreman asked where I had been the previous night. I said that I had been rostered a day off, which he refuted, and when we both looked at the roster, I should have booked on at 11.45 p.m. the previous day to my turning up for duty. The foreman allowed me to clock on for duty, but wanted me to write a report to explain my absence.

A picture taken in 1967 of the Wild-West-style carriages that were left in the Mitcham yard after working the evening staff train from the Islington Workshops. Waving to the camera is my brother Ken, on the left, with me (then aged fourteen) on the right. Above Ken's waving hand can be seen an emergency brake valve that would have been used by the guard or shunter to slow or halt a reversing movement if necessary.

An English Electric 800-class locomotive rounding the curve at Mile End Junction with a small string of oil tank wagons from Port Adelaide in 1969. Directly above the coupler between loco and wagon is a re-railing ramp, used in case of small derailments in shunting yards. This kind of locomotive was often used on the Islington to Mitcham staff train at the time.

The way the internal mail system worked, meant that the main office in Adelaide did not receive my report until the 15th April. A couple of days later, there was a letter waiting for me, and on reading it, you would have thought that I had committed a heinous crime. It stated that I had broken the rule regarding leave without permission and that I was late in submitting my report. I had apparently laid myself open to suspension and dismissal, even though I had only misread the roster. I was told that I would not be paid for the time lost, which was to be expected. Harsh times indeed!

In the first week of June 1970, there was an interesting letter waiting for me at work. From the 16th June, I was to be transferred to Snowtown until further notice. This was to enable a fireman there to have a week's leave, but I secretly suspected it was a form of punishment for the previous episode of my absence. As it turned out, I was only there for seven days before being transferred back to Mile End. While at Snowtown, my shifts were fairly lenient. I was to book on at Mile End to work forward to Snowtown, and then sign on every other day at two o'clock in the morning. I had to stay in barracks for the duration, but this gave me an opportunity to have a look around Snowtown in the daylight for a change, as quite often we only passed by in the darkness of night.

Snowtown was located 89¾ miles north of Adelaide on the main Adelaide to Port Pirie line, and had a small population of about 500. Its location, on a fertile plain between the Mount Lofty Ranges and the Barunga Range, was in an area ideal for wheat growing and sheep grazing, and a township was established there in 1869, formally being recognised in 1878. Its main street was Fourth Street, which boasted a large general store and a memorial hall. Years later, in 1999, the town became notorious for being the site of Australia's largest serial killing. A number of bodies were discovered in barrels, hidden in the town's disused bank vaults!

From the railway perspective, it was also a junction station for four lines - to Wallaroo on the west coast of the Yorke Peninsula, to Brinkworth on the Gladstone main line in the east, towards Port Pirie in the north and of course south to Adelaide via Bowmans. The lines to Wallaroo and Brinkworth were worked under the Train Order method of working. A locomotive was usually based at Snowtown to work the once-a-week train from the five-mile branch line at nearby Lochiel. Its traffic was mainly salt from the Bumbunga Lake. The working was made by a two-way Train Order, as there were no train control phones at Lochiel.

Whilst I was based at Snowtown, I was rostered to work a train from there to Gladstone, *via* Brinkworth. This was considered a local job, so I never normally would have had the chance to work this kind of train, being based at Mile End. I signed on using the appearance sheet at the Snowtown Station Master's office at 02:00 Thursday morning, and worked train number 113, the 03:00 goods to Gladstone. On our arrival at 06:40, I was able to make use of the local bakery that luckily opened early to cater for railway staff, to buy a hot pie and an iced finger bun! By the time we got back to Snowtown we had been on duty for more than eleven hours! Gladstone was another unusual station, being graced with three different gauges in the late sixties, though the narrow gauge was being used less often.

Gladstone was a junction station on the main Port Pirie to Broken Hill main line. The narrow gauge line ran to Wilmington, which eventually closed in March 1990. The station at Gladstone was always a hive of activity, being used to load grain as well as sheep. It even boasted a coaling tower for steam locomotive servicing. The broad gauge ran a daily Bluebird railcar service from Adelaide to Gladstone, but this service ceased in 1982. These railcars sometimes towed a refrigerated boxcar that was painted the same blue-and-silver colour scheme to match the railcars.

Once my stay was finished at Snowtown, I was rostered to work back to Mile End on a freight train. On the way, we had to call in at Dry Creek to detach a few wagons. It was my job to climb down to speak to the signalman at the Dry Creek cabin on the telephone, to gain permission to operate the points that would cross our train over the main line and into the Dry Creek yard. The procedure should have gone quite smoothly; I should

25

The rugged scenery to be found in the Mount Lofty Ranges. This location is between Sleeps Hill tunnel and Eden Hills station on the South Line, where a ruling gradient of 1 in 45 exists. The course of the original railway can be seen at the bottom left of the picture, where the tracks used to cross a large viaduct. CALLAN DAVIES

have unlocked the switch indicator padlock using my 'S' key, (kept permanently around my neck on a piece of ribbon), spoke to the signalman, reversed the points, and then waved the train past the signal which would have returned to the stop position, climbing aboard as the train moved by.

The guard would have reversed the points once we were in clear of the main line; one of the reasons that a guard's brake van was always placed at the rear of a train. In reality it went something like this: I clambered down and unlocked the points, spoke to the signalman who replied "Be quick, as I have a down Peterborough railcar due soon." I then attempted to lift and turn the handle of the switch indicator, and it wouldn't budge. The driver (a Snowtown man) peered down from the cab and enquired what was taking so long. He was not much help, considering I had not had much practical experience at doing this kind of thing. He just tutted impatiently. With this, a 250-class Bluebird railcar whizzed passed us, travelling in the opposite direction. The Down Peterborough! Of course; the presence of this train on the track circuits was preventing me from unlocking the points! After this, everything went like clockwork. When I climbed back into the cab and explained that I hadn't done much of that kind of thing before, he just shrugged his shoulders and stated something along the lines that as I was 'fresh out of the school' I should know the job inside out!

The railways in South Australia, including the Commonwealth standard gauge system, utilised a method of working known as Train Order Working. Under this method of operation, train movements on single lines were authorised by a written order that was dictated by telephone directly from the train controller. Train Control centres on the broad gauge were located at Adelaide and Murray Bridge, with a train Control office situated at Mount Gambier in the southeast of the state. A Train Order was a pink slip of paper that was officially known as form number 377 and measured approximately 8¼ inches tall by 5½ inches wide. Upon this was written operating instructions that were usually directed to the driver and guard of any given train. In Train Order Territory, every train movement was governed by the issuing of these orders, but, as already mentioned, Train Orders could be issued elsewhere, for example, the failure of an Absolute Three-Position signal. Supplies of these orders, in book form, were kept in signal cabins, stationmaster's offices, and in Train Control telephone cabinets.

When a Train Order was being received from the Controller, the instructions were written down in ink on the Order form during transmission. As many copies as required could be made simultaneously using the double-faced carbon paper provided, but the usual number was three; one for the driver, one for the guard, and the original that was kept at the location where the order was received. The information that Train Control dictated over the telephone consisted of the following:-

- The date
- The Order number (which ran consecutively and started with 'one' from midnight each day)
- The train number (as shown in the Working Time Table)
- The locomotive or railcar number
- The station name where the order was received

This information was then followed by the instructions that Control wanted the train crew to be in possession of; for example, "Proceed to Sandergrove - Take Passing Siding and cross Passenger 340, car number 255 - then Proceed to Goolwa." This was then followed by the time that the order was

The slip of paper used to inform staff of their temporary transfer to another station.

transmitted and the Controller's name.

While the Controller was dictating the Train Order, he also wrote out a copy in ink on his own Train Order book. Once the message was completed, the person receiving the dictation must verbally repeat the order back to the Controller word for word. On Train Order Territory, the person repeating the order must clearly pronounce the station names then spell them letter for letter. The same must be done with numbers. As the employee was doing this, the Controller was underlining the order word for word on his copy. Once the order was repeated back, the person must tell the Controller their name and the time the order was repeated back. The spelling-out was a slow process but it ensured that no misunderstandings or mistakes were made. Should a mistake be made by the person making out a Train Order, the word 'CANCELLED' must be written across the face of the order which must be left in the book; no alterations, erasures, or writing between the lines was permitted. On Electric Staff or Three-Position Territory, the Train Order was repeated back, clearly pronouncing station names and numbers, without the spelling-out process.

Once the writing of the order was completed, the original was filed away and each copy was handed respectively to the guard and driver, who were to thoroughly read it to make sure that they understood every detail. The driver must show the order to his fireman, who must peruse it thoroughly, then place it in such a position in the cab so that both men could see it. Some locomotives were fitted with a fixed clipboard for this purpose. If either member of the crew did not fully understand the Train Order's instructions, the train was not to proceed until the misunderstanding was rectified.

On Train Order Territory, Orders were issued for the following reasons:-

- For a train to enter a section
- For trains to cross or pass on the same route at either terminal or intermediate stations
- For trains that were crossing or passing at a station where Train Order territory ends and another system of working starts
- For a through train that was to cross or pass, at an intermediate station, another train that terminated its journey at that station; the order indicated that the terminating train had arrived and completed its movement

GOODS TRAIN SERVICES
GLADSTONE AND WALLAROO, via BUTE
DOWN

Train Order System under Train Control between Gladstone and Wallaroo.

			Tues., Thurs., Sat.
			113
— 45¾	SNOWTOWN★∧ CJWX Condowie .... UX	dep arr	a m 3 00 —
52	Brinkworth .... CJOWX	dep arr	3 30
— 84	GLADSTONE ☐CEJOF WX	dep arr	4 00 6 40

MONDAYS TO SATURDAYS—UP

Miles from Gladstone	Stations	Thurs., Sat.	Tues.,
		458	728
—	GLADSTONE .... dep	a m 8 30	p m 5 30
32	Brinkworth .... arr "	11 45	8 45
38½	Condowie .... dep arr	12 35pm	9 35
45	SNOWTOWN.......... dep arr	— 1 30	— 10 30
—	" .... dep	2 35	11 35

(columns marked "To Mile End")

USE OF CANE HOOPS FOR TRAIN ORDERS
hoops will be used at Kadina and Bute to deliver train orders to train crews working Trains. Care must be taken to see that Train Orders are correctly attached to the d carefully handled to avoid damage. Train crews must remove the orders and throw out the hoops to allow recovery by Station Staff.

SAR 5963/62

An excerpt from the SAR
Working Time Table giving the timings for the freight trains that I worked as a fireman whilst temporarily being based at Snowtown.

A train was never allowed to enter an occupied block, except to assist a disabled train. The Train Order was issued to the relief train only when the exact location of the failed train was known.

At some stations within Train Order Territory, equipment known as Train Order Signals were situated within the station yard,

The view from the level crossing at Snowtown, looking down Fourth Street, the main shopping thoroughfare in the town. Note the RX painted on the road to make car drivers aware of the railway crossing ahead.

One of the RBp-class (Refrigerated, Bogie, passenger) insulated vans used with the Bluebird 250-class railcars sits at Gladstone waiting for the return trip back to Adelaide. Note the station sign, which states 'Change here for Wilmington, Adelaide, Pt. Pirie, and Peterborough'. Note also that the van is equipped with two different braking systems; the single pipe next to the coupler is for loco-hauled use, while the two pipes on the left were used with the railcars.

The trackside view of Snowtown station. Note that there is no platform provided here. The signal in the background, adjacent to the station building, is a Train Order signal. These purely indicated to the driver whether he was to stop for orders, slow for orders or that the station was closed.

Shown above is the controversial image used originally as a fridge magnet, designed by a local shopkeeper in Snowtown. The locals and relatives of the deceased were furious about this, but the un-named biker who wore this T-shirt could not see the harm in it as, in his words, the murders were actually committed elsewhere.

This is an example of a switch indicator as used by the SAR in the 1960s, similar to the one I attempted to use at Dry Creek. The location of this indicator was the northern end of Virginia station. This was locked electrically by a local track circuit and would have needed the use of an Outlying Switch Lock before the handle could be raised to operate the points.

A view from Snowtown yard as the East-West from Adelaide arrives on the main line to cross its counterpart standing in the passing siding with 901 in charge. Between the two locomotives, nestling between the trees, can be seen the Snowtown barracks where I spent a week in June 1970.
BRIAN R BANDT

yard, usually at or near the controlling signal cabin or Station Master's office. These signals differed from other fixed signals in that they had round-ended arms and did not control movements of trains. Their sole purpose was to indicate to a driver whether Train Orders were to be picked up. The arm was placed to the left of the mast (as viewed from an approaching train), and for signals that were to face both directions, two arms were placed on the same mast. These signals were used to indicate the following to drivers:-

• Stop for orders, (arm horizontal)
• Slow for orders, (arm raised 45°)
• The station is open but there are no orders, (arm raised 90°)
• The station is closed, (arm raised 90° and yellow disc on mast).

The normal indication shown by the Train Order signal was horizontal, and when the driver challenged the signal with the locomotive code whistle of four short blasts (Call for Train Order signal), the signal was raised to forty-five or ninety degrees as appropriate. When the station was closed for the day, a yellow disc was placed on the mast. The night indications were the same as normal semaphore signals, red light for the horizontal position, yellow for forty-five degrees, and green for ninety degrees. The yellow disc was capable of displaying a yellow light at night. Once a train had received its Train Order to proceed, the Signalman or Station Master raised the Train Order signal to the ninety-degree position. When the guard had received and understood his copy of the order, he was to observe that the Train Order signal was raised before signalling to the driver that the train may start. Once the train had departed, the Train Order signal was immediately returned to the stop position.

Should a non-stopping train be signalled to 'Slow for Orders', the driver was to reduce the train's speed to eight miles-per-hour to enable his fireman and guard to pick up the Train Orders as the train passed through. This was significantly slower than when exchanging Electric Staffs by hand (15mph), considering one was giving and receiving staffs at the same time. Cane hoops were sometimes utilised for delivering orders on the move by hand. The instruction to train crews was to remove the order promptly and throw out the hoop to allow recovery by the station staff. Whilst on the subject of cane hoops, I had a funny experience whilst exchanging an Electric Staff this way.

One could never be sure, at some stations, whether the staff was to be exchanged by hand or automatic exchanger. The location of the exchanger at night was given by a white light, and through experience one could tell by its position whether this was going to be by hand or not. On this particular occasion we were returning from Port Pirie with a freight train one night. I had buckled up the staff in the metal hoop ready for the auto exchanger, when the driver commented that the guy was on the platform ready to change by hand! I frantically swapped the staff into the cane hoop and opened the cab door behind the driver, while he was reducing the train's speed accordingly. The man on the platform was shining his torch in my direction to pinpoint where my staff was being held, but shone the light into my eyes. I quickly grabbed at the hoop he was offering me, but suddenly realised that I still had the other staff! In a panic I threw out the other staff onto the ground, desperately checking that I'd retained the correct one. I could picture the Station Master spending the next half an hour trying to find the discarded staff in the darkness.

Broad gauge lines in South Australia that were worked under the Train Order system are listed below:-

• Mount Gambier to Millicent
• Wolseley to Mount Gambier
• Mount Barker Junction to Victor Harbour
• Wallaroo to Snowtown and Brinkworth
• Riverton to Spalding
• Hamley Bridge to Balaklava, Brinkworth and Gladstone
• Bowmans to Moonta
• Roseworthy to Morgan
• Nuriootpa to Truro

A typical country station scene with a Train Order signal indicating that the station was closed for the day. This was shown by the disc halfway up the mast being rotated to face approaching trains. This particular station was located in the south-east of South Australia on the Mount Gambier to Millicent branch line.

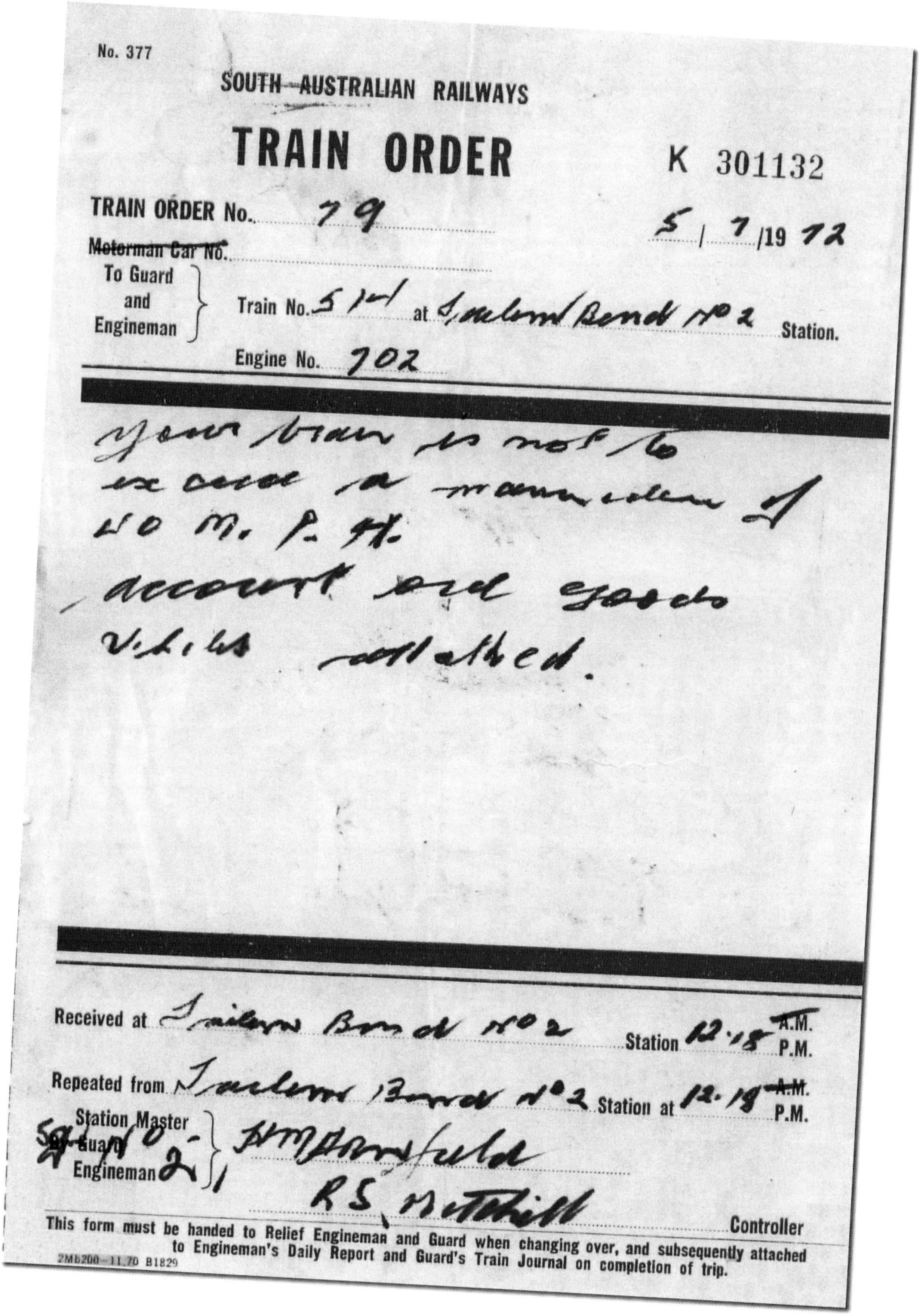

No. 377

SOUTH AUSTRALIAN RAILWAYS

TRAIN ORDER

K 301132

TRAIN ORDER No. *79*

5 | 7 /19 72

Motorman Car No. ....

To Guard and Engineman } Train No. *51d* at *Tailem Bend Nº 2* Station.

Engine No. *702*

Your train is not to exceed a maximum of 40 M. P. H. account ord goods vehicles attached.

Received at *Tailem Bend Nº 2* Station *12·18* A.M. P.M.

Repeated from *Tailem Bend Nº 2* Station at *12·19* A.M. P.M.

Station Master or Guard Engineman } *H M Dransfield*

R S Mitchill

Controller

This form must be handed to Relief Engineman and Guard when changing over, and subsequently attached to Engineman's Daily Report and Guard's Train Journal on completion of trip.

2M6200—11.70 B1829

Shown actual size is an example of a Train Order that indicates the general layout of Form 377, as it was officially known. This particular Order was issued in Three-Position Automatic Signal Territory, and received by the signalman at Tailem Bend Number Two cabin, for a passenger train and reads, "Your train is not to exceed a maximum of 40 MPH account ord (ordinary) goods vehicles attached." This was probably to get urgent perishable freight to Adelaide rather than delaying it for the next goods train.

A fireman's life on a diesel locomotive was not much easier than on a steam loco. The only difference was the fact that there was no more shovelling tons of coal and keeping thirsty boilers full of water. As well as keeping a sharp lookout for the driver (especially on 'hood' locomotives where the view ahead was somewhat restricted), the fireman had to let trains in and out of passing sidings, collect Electric Staffs or Train Orders, make frequent checks inside the engine rooms, as well as making the tea when time permitted. On mainline locos, there was an additional task of keeping an eye on the vigilance device. This device was an air operated system that kept the loco crew alert.

Air slowly built up pressure to a certain point where an air operated whistle started to sound. If left alone, this whistle would issue a piercing shriek, then apply the train's brakes. The fireman's job was to cancel this by pressing a button that was located just under the side cab window. The process would then start all over again. The whole idea of having two people in the cab was to ensure that each could keep an eye on each other so that no-one nodded off to sleep. Believe me, some of the night

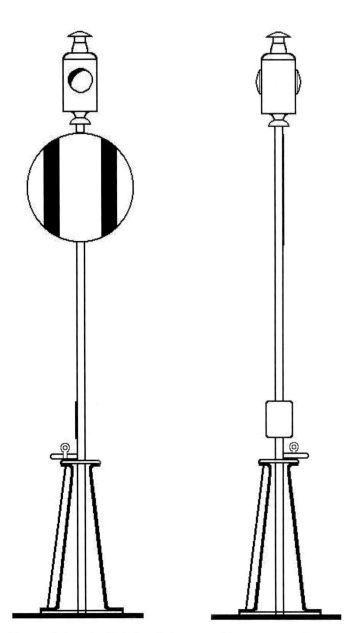

Illustrated above is a Train Stop Indicator, used by passengers where trains were booked to stop as required. The small plate near the operating handle instructed passengers to 'Lift the pin and rotate the handle through ninety degrees.' The left-hand view is what the driver would see on the approach to the station, whereas the right-hand view is the indicator in its normal position.
SAR / STATE TRANSPORT AUTHORITY HERITAGE COLLECTION

jobs could be quite tedious, and there was many an occasion that my eyelids started to droop.

In my early days as an acting fireman on the mainline, I was keen to give a good impression. One occasion springs to mind regarding the making of a can of tea. We had stopped at some remote place like Kallora to change Electric Staffs, so I asked the driver if he fancied a cup of tea. His reply was rather non-committal, so I hopped out with my billy-can to obtain some water from the station's rain-water tank. This was the only supply of water that some of these stations had. I twisted the tank's tap - nothing. I twisted the tap the opposite way - nothing. The tank was obviously bone dry, so I returned to the cab with the Electric Staff and an empty can. The driver's wry smile indicated that he probably guessed that this was going to be the case.

Not all jobs were long ones; sometimes we worked jobs known as 'working to cross'. This would involve setting out from Mile End until we 'met' a given train that was travelling in the opposite direction. On paper this would have been at a given location, but sometimes this varied wildly due to late running and so on. I remember working one of these jobs one winter's night, and our meeting point was to be Balyarta, a remote siding in the middle of nowhere with no platform, 41½ miles southeast of Adelaide. The weather was atrocious, pouring down with rain, as we drew our locomotives alongside the other waiting freight train. We each clambered onto our respective trains and then drew further into the 'yard' to enable the guards to do the same. I felt sorry for them, as they had a lot further to walk in the pouring rain than we had.

The SAR utilised end to end radio on certain South Line trains to ease communication between enginemen and guards on long trains. The system used rather bulky portable radio sets that were only fitted to mainline locomotives of the 900 and 930-class diesels, and 8300-class goods brake vans and CE-class passenger brake vans. The use of these radios made the starting of very long freight trains a lot easier and safer. Previously, guards had to reduce the train's brake pipe pressure as a pre-arranged signal that the train was ready to depart, especially when the guard was out of sight at some locations, like the remote station of Balyarta, which was in a cutting. As mentioned at the beginning of this chapter, the location of the equipment in the 900-class locomotives left a lot to be desired - directly above the cover for the Electric Staff exchanger. A typical message from the guard, once he had physically given the driver his loading information and returned to his brakevan, might sound something like this: "To the driver of train number 969, diesel number 903, you can draw down to the stick, and we're ready to go when you're right," which meant that when he was ready, the driver could ease his train towards the signal, and once he received a proceed aspect, he was "right away" (alright to proceed).

At certain stations, some trains were listed in the public timetable to stop "if required". If one was already on the train concerned, a quick word to the guard was needed to make sure that the train stopped where you required. If you were on the station waiting to flag the train down, a special piece of equipment was provided on the platform for this very purpose and was known as a Train Stop Indicator. These indicators were another piece of equipment that appeared as if they came straight from the American Wild West. A small cast plate on the post of the indicator gave the instructions as follows: "To stop a train, lift the pin and rotate the handle through ninety degrees." When turned to face an approaching train, they displayed a white circular disc with two vertical black stripes by day and a white light above the disc by night. The light and disc were not visible to the approaching train in their normal position. Only trains scheduled as a conditional stop in the Working Timetable would stop when the disc or light was displayed to the driver. It was part of the guard's duty to return the indicator to the normal position before re-starting his train.

The fireman and guard from the East-West Express go to exchange the Electric Staff at Kallora, a block station 52 miles 52 chains north of Adelaide on the main Port Pirie line. Note the infamous water tank that I tried to obtain water from without success.

A timeless view of 930-class Goodwin-Alco, class leader number 930 in ex-works condition, on the 85-foot electric turntable at Victor Harbour. This turntable was still required due to the single-cabbed nature of the first six units of this class of locomotive, as well as the ten 900-class locos. The plug next to the headlight on this locomotive was for the jumper cable for multiple unit working.
AUSTRALIAN RAILWAY HISTORICAL SOCIETY, SA DIVISION.

Views from the Cab

A classic example of why two people were required in the cab of an 830-class Alco 'hood' locomotive when working long-end-first. Here we see a 900-class loco framed in the window of an 830 Alco at Adelaide's Gaol Loop Junction in March 1978.

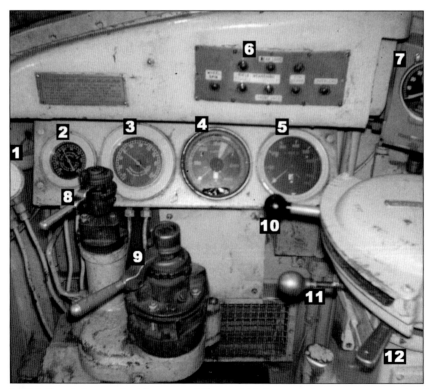

Cab controls of the 900-class English Electric locomotive. They are as follows:- 1, Vigilance Device Pressure gauge; 2, Independent Brake Cylinder Pressure gauge; 3, Automatic Brake Pressure gauge; 4, Main Generator Ammeter gauge; 5, Dynamic Brake Ammeter; 6, Driver's Indicator Lights; 7, Hasler Speedometer and Timepiece; 8, Independent Brake Valve Handle; 9, Automatic Brake Valve Handle; 10, Power Controller Handle; 11, Reverser Handle; 12, Master Switch.

To operate the dynamic brake on these locomotives, a latch was operated with the power handle in notch '0', allowing the handle to be pushed forward to positions B, L, or D. When accelerating a train away from a standing start, once ten miles per hour had been reached, the throttle could be opened straight to notch ten, providing the train load was not too heavy. In notch ten the automatic Load Regulator came into use, regulating the electrical current to prevent the main generator from becoming overloaded.

Cab view of the tall steel trestle bridge over the River Light on the southerly approach to Hamley Bridge station. Hamley Bridge was a junction station for the Gladstone line via Balaklava, and Peterborough *via* Riverton.

Arriving at Roseworthy station from Adelaide, on the way to Peterborough. Adjacent to the Train Order signal, through the window, the signalman can be seen crossing his arms to indicate that we were to cross another train here. Just down the line, our next signal is indicating that we can proceed down to the section signal at medium speed. Note the water column at the end of the Down platform. The tree trunk in the foreground is the base of a very tall palm tree!

Approaching Adelaide's Torrens Bridge Junction on the Up Port Adelaide line, we meet a freight train headed by a single 930-class Alco number 965, running from Mile End to Dry Creek. Considering that we had received a caution aspect at the previous signal, there is not a lot of room for error should the driver inadvertently pass the signal at danger! The walls of Adelaide Gaol can be seen on the right.

Mile End driver Roger Sallis takes a well-earned 'crib' break at the Mile End North Arrival yard between trips to and from Port Adelaide's Gillman Yard, with 830-class Alco number 843, in March 1978. The short nose on these locomotives housed the Westinghouse air brake equipment and the crew toilet.

Hauled Passenger Trains

The Broken Hill Express glides through Islington station on its way to Terowie in the 1960s. At Terowie, this train would connect with the narrow gauge service to Peterborough, then forward to eastern states via Broken Hill.
SAR / STATE TRANSPORT AUTHORITY HERITAGE COLLECTION

The Overland Express struggles with the 1 in 50 gradient between Eden Hills and Blackwood with two 900-class diesel-electric locomotives at the head. Note that both units are facing forward rather than back-to-back. The first car behind the locomotive was an old wooden clerestory-roofed car jointly owned by the South Australian and Victorian Railways, and would have been used as a wayside car for picking up passengers en route.
SAR / STATE TRANSPORT AUTHORITY HERITAGE COLLECTION

The 16:20 service from Adelaide to Tailem Bend, train number 701, is seen just after leaving Adelaide in 1969. This service ran Mondays to Thursdays only. On Fridays, it departed at 18:15 as train number 801, and would have connected with a road bus service to Pinnaroo at Tailem Bend. I am sure the crew have settled down with a billy-can of tea for the 75 mile journey ahead.

The Blue Lake Express prepares to leave Mount Gambier at 08:10 in the morning for its 305-mile journey to Adelaide in 1969. Note that the front of the locomotive does not have the silver chevron painted on it.

A triple-headed Overland Express passes through the eastern slopes of the Mount Lofty Ranges near Yantaringa with ageing 900-class locomotives at the head. Note the Motorail facility attached behind the locos.
BRIAN R BANDT

Number 900 herself, *Lady Norrie*, sits at Victor Harbour waiting to return to Adelaide with an Easter excursion on 3rd April 1972. The train consisted of twelve cars and weighed 417 tons!
BRIAN R BANDT

The East-West Express speeds across the plains on the northern approach to Snowtown in June 1970. Although the train seems to have a reasonable consist, it was unusual for the train to be double-headed. Note the very basic road warning sign for the level crossing; the only notice usually taken of these signs were for rifle target practice!

The Overland Express makes its final approach to Murray Bridge over the Burdett Pastures early in the morning on its way from Melbourne to Adelaide in 1978, when the author made a return trip back to South Australia for a four-week visit.

Refreshment Stops

A 1960s picture of the 08:00 morning train from Adelaide to Mount Gambier, pausing at Murray Bridge for a fifteen-minute refreshment stop. Some of these railcars were eventually modified to accommodate a buffet facility. Murray Bridge was the boundary between the Adelaide Division and the Murray Bridge Division.

Train number 255, the 07:35 morning passenger service from Adelaide to Port Pirie, pauses at Bowmans station for a refreshment stop for 20 minutes. This also gave the crew a chance for a cup of tea or a bite to eat.

Accidents

Two photographs of the twin 900s damaged by a collision with a wine truck on an unprotected level crossing near Rowland Flat in South Australia's Barossa Valley region, on 26th March 1974. The train struck the trailer of the road vehicle which ended up in a nearby field. Luckily no-one was injured in this incident, but it took two days to clear the line.
BRIAN R BANDT

Train Designation Discs. You will have noticed in most of the photographs, a small square disc placed on the front of trains. These were known as designation discs and were used to indicate destinations to signalmen and other staff as follows:-

SOUTH, between Adelaide, Mitcham, Blackwood, Belair and Bridgewater.

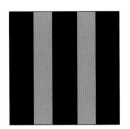

OUTER HARBOUR, between Adelaide, Port Dock, Semaphore and Outer Harbour.

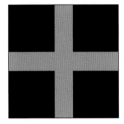

NORTH, between Adelaide, Islington Northfield, Penfield, Gawler and North Gawler.

FINSBURY, between Adelaide, and Finsbury.

WILLUNGA , between Adelaide, Brighton, Marino and Willunga.

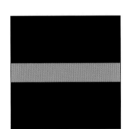

GRANGE, between Adelaide, Holden's, Hendon and Grange.

A new 830-class loco stands outside the shed at Mile End Diesel Depot attached to a dynamometer car, with the fresh paintwork glistening in the afternoon sun. This loco was on its delivery run and was destined for the new standard gauge, working between Port Pirie and Broken Hill. If my memory serves me correctly, this loco was fitted with a Davies and Metcalf brake valve instead of the usual Westinghouse.

CHAPTER IV
All Change

My short career with the South Australian Railways eventually came to an official end on the 25th July 1970, when my parents finally decided to return to Britain. This decision had put me on the spot in a number of ways. My career had been starting to take off, I was saving up to buy a motorcycle to get to and from work, and I had a steady girlfriend. On the other side of the coin, I had not seen any of my relatives for over eleven years, all of whom lived in England. My Nan had already suffered a stroke, so my parents had their minds set on returning as soon as possible. It was hinted at that I could return to Australia on my own, once I had turned eighteen, if I did not like life in England. I had put this scenario to the railways on my final interview in Adelaide, and they were prepared to put my career position on hold for a maximum of two years.

With this in mind, I boarded the 'Overland Express' amid a tearful farewell to some of my old school friends who had turned up to wave me goodbye, to make my final railway journey from Adelaide to Melbourne. Nearly 2½ hours and 60¼ miles later, when we stopped at Murray Bridge for the customary refreshment break, I went up to the front to have a chat with the loco crew. When they realised that this was my last trip, I was honoured that they allowed me to be the acting fireman between Murray Bridge and Tailem Bend. Although this part of the journey was in darkness, it was also shrouded in heavy fog; not surprising, as we were running parallel to the north-eastern banks of the River Murray. There was no missing this boat, as

we arrived in Melbourne the next morning a whole day before our Chandris Lines' ship, the *Australis*, was due to sail for Southampton. The month of August was spent crossing the vast Pacific Ocean and it seemed strange to experience two Monday the 10th of Augusts as we crossed the International Dateline!

We eventually arrived in Southampton to find the ship's holds contained three feet of water as well as the luggage! We later found that this particular ship seemed to suffer from some kind of jinx, as it had caught fire during a previous cruise. It was almost five hours after docking that we were allowed to disembark, and we were met by my Uncle who lived in Andover. We travelled to his house by coach (well, he was a bus enthusiast) and stayed there overnight. My first taste of British Railways came the next morning when we caught an Exeter to Waterloo service, hauled by a diesel-hydraulic 'Warship' locomotive. After transferring to the Central Line Underground in London, we arrived in Epping in the early afternoon and, with the distinctive smell of creosoted sleepers in the air, all of my childhood memories came flooding back. All that was needed was a red 'RT' double-decker bus waiting outside to have completed the picture. The only thing that seemed to have changed were the colour of the trains - they were silver instead of the familiar red. Also missing was the lingering smell of coal gas from the nearby gasworks.

The family settled in with relatives as a temporary measure until we found permanent housing and thoughts were turned

A 1970s scene at Epping station on the London Underground Central line. The car park on the left is where the goods yard and engine shed were located during LNER days.

to employment. I had already heard about crack expresses such as the 'Flying Scotsman', and the high-speed feats of locomotives like *Mallard* on the East Coast Main Line. I knew that King's Cross was the London terminus for this main line to Scotland and I had heard of Stratford's reputation as the largest depot in Britain, both of which were in the Eastern Region. My knowledge of London's local geography let me down though, as I did not realise that Stratford did not supply locomotives for King's Cross services. It seemed that my family would settle somewhere near Epping, and as Stratford was on the Central line, a straightforward journey from Epping, I made my enquiries there about becoming a train driver. Again, I heard the general consensus from family friends that the chances of obtaining a driving job were like finding gold dust, but within a fortnight, I was given an interview and aptitude test.

The railway system that I was about to start work with was coming to the end of the 1955 Modernisation Plan. Apparently, approximately one-and-a-half million pounds had been invested by the Government over a 15-year period to the newly formed British Railways. This had nationalised the Big Four companies, Great Western, the London and North Eastern, London Midland and Scottish, and Southern Railway, and in 1970, was attaining a new corporate identity that would be known simply as British Rail. A new logo was devised, consisting of a double arrow symbol that pointed in opposite directions. Some wag suggested that this was a sure sign that the railways didn't know in which direction it was heading. Diesel locomotives that had been wearing a two-tone green livery, were painted in an all-over blue colour, with yellow ends

for higher visibility to track workers.

The financial position of the railways in 1970 was still worsening, despite the substantial line closures of the 1960s under the orders of Richard Beeching, the British Railways Board chairman. This was beginning to show with some of the steam-era rolling stock that was still in use, and the fact that wagons and locomotives still used screw couplings and buffers as well as vacuum brakes; I was used to trains having automatic couplers and air brakes as standard. I could not believe that a railway that was capable of running trains at 100 miles per hour still lived in the dark ages as far as simple things like couplings were concerned. It was generally accepted that the automatic, or 'buckeye' couplers, were stronger and better at keeping derailed vehicles upright than conventional screw couplings.

I was even more surprised to learn that many freight trains were running around where the only brakes were on the locomotive or the guard's handbrake in the brake van.

Picture the scene; if a screw coupling broke on the unbraked portion of a train whilst travelling uphill, the only way of stopping the runaway rear portion would be for the guard to furiously wind on a hand-brake on a twenty-ton brake van! That was if he was paying attention in the first place.

This practice would have been a total 'no-no' in Australia, except in emergencies. We even had to 'pipe up' vehicles if a shunt had to be made from a yard onto a main line. British brake vans on freight trains were more like a garden shed on wheels in appearance, and as to comfort, forget it! They were not even equipped with any internal lighting. The railways obviously did

> All of my childhood memories came flooding back. All that was needed was a red 'RT' double-decker bus waiting outside to have completed the picture.

The view from Epping station looking north-east in 1970. A train is arriving from Ongar, passing under the very bridge that I used to watch the steam trains from back in 1958. The old water tank was still in existence! Note also the disc distant signal facing the train on the right of the picture. Sadly, the Central Line no longer runs services through to Ongar from Epping.

Shown above are two examples of goods brake vans that were once in use in Britain. The similarity to a 'shed on wheels' is evident in these pictures. The one at the top is a 20 ton four-wheeled version, as used by the Midland Region, whilst the one below is a 25 ton Southern Region example with bogies and a continuous vacuum brake system. This one would have been capable of running at 60mph. The box on the side of the body was the guard's lookout window, equivalent to the raised cupola on American and Australian brake vans.

not want the guard to get too comfortable.

The promotional ladder to becoming a driver basically followed the same pattern as I was already used to; cleaner, fireman, and driver. During my time as a cleaner, I learned about various diesels that were based at Stratford. English Electric was a very familiar name, but now I was being introduced to names like Brush/Sulzer and British Thompson Houston. Stratford was also the home for diesel DMUs that were powered by British Universal Traction engines, as well as the familiar Rolls Royce engines. I soon discovered that many operational practices worked on the nod-and-wink principle. If no more work was to be found for the day, we were allowed to go home early without any official clocking off. This was most alien to me as I was used to the very regimented way of working in Australia. Needless to say, I soon got the hang of it.

On making casual weekend observations at Liverpool Street station, I smiled to myself as I noticed an age-old tradition still being carried out - that of allowing the fireman to have a drive when moving locomotives from the servicing point to the waiting train in the platform. In my opinion, that was the only way to enable trainee drivers to learn the job.

The Stratford area was a hive of railway activity in 1970. The depot area itself was contained within a circle of running lines and contained many large buildings (see map on page 49). The running shed, known simply as 'B' and 'C' shed, sat on the site of what was originally called the Jubilee Shed, but took up only a quarter of its original size. This was where the basic maintenance was carried out, including cleaning. Next to this was a large brick building, known as the diesel repair shop, or DRS for short, where heavier maintenance took place, including wheel turning on a special lathe. This process literally shaved the wheel treads to eliminate flat spots caused by wheel skid. Stratford was one of the few depots to be graced with such a machine, which meant that locomotives from other depots often visited to have their wheels 'turned'. To the southeast of the DRS was 'A' shed, where maintenance was carried out on Stratford's allocation of DMUs. This shed was the original home to diesel locomotives during the changeover from steam traction in the 1960s. Dotted about the depot yard were various buildings that dated back to the steam age, and one of these housed the breakdown crane. This building, for some reason, was known as the New Shed, even though it was one of the oldest buildings on the depot.

Between this and the main running shed sat a row of grimy buildings, black with the soot of time, that housed a number of rooms and offices. This included the office for the Depot Master, the administration offices and roster clerks, as well as the clothing stores, where uniforms were issued. These stores consisted of a couple of dingy rooms stacked to the ceiling with various garments that made up our uniform. This was new to me as a loco man, as I never had to wear a uniform before, only a set of overalls. The procedure for obtaining anything from these stores was like trying to procure something from the black market. One had to take a requisition form to the counter and then sign a receipt for the goods that were handed over. This was easier said than done. Even though the shelves were straining under their loads, they never seemed to have what anyone wanted. "Come and see me at the end of the week and I'll see what I can do" was the usual response.

It was within this same shabby building that I began my training to become what was beginning to be called a Driver's Assistant, instead of 'fireman'. This initial induction training, as it was called, was carried out by an ex-driver named Jack Searle. His hobby was railway photography, and he made this pay by selling some of his work to trainspotters at King's Cross station on Saturday mornings. During this period of training, I was to learn all about semaphore and colour-light signals, especially four-aspect signalling. Where three-aspect signalling would progressively slow a driver by showing green, yellow, then red signals, four-aspect signalling would show a sequence of green, two yellows, one yellow, then red. This was very useful where the line speed was high and the two-yellow aspect was known as a preliminary caution. I also learned about another safety feature, known as Automatic Warning System (A.W.S.), associated with fixed signals. This was a totally new thing for me and was quite interesting.

The main feature was a receiver under the cab of a traction unit, and a double-box magnet arrangement placed on the track, between the running rails, about two hundred yards on the approach to the fixed signal that it applied to. This on-track box housed a permanent and electro-magnet. When the associated signal showed a green aspect, the electro-magnet became energised and when a traction unit that was equipped with A.W.S passed over the magnets, a bell would sound in the cab for about a second and this would indicate to the driver that the signal was green. If the signal showed a cautionary or danger aspect, the electro-magnet became de-energised and a horn would sound in the train's cab. This would require cancelling by the driver and, if he failed to do so within about five seconds, the brakes would automatically be applied. This system was considered safe in that if the electro-magnet ever became de-energised for whatever reason, the horn would sound within the cab. The AWS system was an aid to drivers in very foggy weather, alerting a driver to signal aspects before he was able to see the actual signal. I noticed a strange thing once I began my duties as a driver's assistant; with the constant sounding of bells at green signals while at work, my subconscious mind started to ignore my alarm clock bell for getting up for early shifts! I was just not used to hearing one-second bell rings all day, and at first, it certainly wasn't conducive to good time-keeping.

Under Jack's guidance, we took advantage of a visit to Fork Junction signal box at Stratford. This little cabin used to control the junction of the line running from Stratford Low Level station through to Temple Mills East. If the reader refers to the map on page 49, this line ran between the Old Yard and the New Shed, effectively cutting the old steam depot in half. In the 1970s, this area was mainly used for container storage and maintenance. When we paid a visit to Fork Junction box, its main use was the signalling of trains into and out of the small siding that was utilised to shunt aside the DMUs on the Stratford to North Woolwich service whilst the driver had his meal break.

We were also shown around the expansive Temple Mills marshalling yards. It was an insight to a place where, more often than not, we would be spending a lot of our working lives.

The row of buildings that greeted anyone visiting the Stratford Locomotive Depot in 1970. The administration offices were on the first floor, and the classroom for trainees was to the left of the entrance where the sign can be seen.

The grimy interior of Stratford's New Shed was the home for the breakdown crane and associated equipment. Attached to the Cowan Sheldon crane is an old Gresley coach, used for the accident van crew.

The central feature of Temple Mills was the hump, the use of which allowed gravity shunting of wagons to approximately 47 roads! Associated with this hump were primary and secondary retarders. These slowed wagons down to acceptable speeds to ensure damage was not caused to other stationary vehicles. The retarders were controlled by a control tower placed next to the hump. Temple Mills was the hub for freight workings in East Anglia, being fed with services from all over Britain. The yard was used to reassemble trains for onward movement to local factories and cold-storage facilities or places like the huge Thames Haven Oil Terminal on the Thames estuary. Trip workings were used to transfer oil wagons or freightliner container vehicles between Temple Mills and Ripple Lane Yard near Dagenham.

Train movements over the shunting hump at Temple Mills were controlled by a three-position upper quadrant semaphore signal. When this signal was raised to 90°, the shunting locos were authorised to start pushing their train towards the hump with the authority of the shunter in charge. When the signal was lowered to 45°, the pushing was to slow down to walking pace to enable the yard staff to uncouple wagons at the top of the hump. Usually, two shunting locomotives coupled together were used to push heavy trains over the shunting hump, with each locomotive being manned by a driver.

I had noticed that all trains carried large numbers on the front. During my initial training, I was to learn that this was known as the Four-Character Train Identification system, which was originally developed in the early 1960s. It was a means of assisting signalmen in identifying trains to enable them to route them correctly. The whole code would identify the class of train, that is Passenger or Freight, and its destination. The first character would show a number from 0 to 9; zero would denote that the train was a light engine (locomotive without a train), 1 was classed as an express passenger train, 2 was a stopping passenger train, whilst a 3 was a parcels train booked to run in excess of 75mph. A number 4 classified the train as an express freight train booked to run at a maximum speed of 75mph (i.e., Freightliner container trains), empty coaching stock trains were classed as a 5, and a 6 was a freight train that was fully fitted with continuous brakes but limited to 60mph. Freight trains that were partially fitted with automatic brakes, where a minimum of half the train's brakes could be operated from the locomotive, were classified as a 7, and were limited to 45mph, and an 8 was a freight train that had only a quarter of the train with continuous brakes, and was usually limited to 35mph. A class 9 train had no continuous brakes at all, the sole braking power being supplied by the locomotive and the guard's brake van. These were usually limited to 35mph or less.

The second character, a letter, denoted the destination area of the train. These differed a little bit, depending on whether the train was starting and terminating within its own division, or travelling further afield into another region altogether. The ones that I would become very familiar with were as follows; the letter D was used on trains that travelled *via* Southbury, usually Hertford services, H was for the area local to Stratford, and K was used on hauled passenger trains *via* Bury St. Edmunds. The letter L was for passenger trains on the Cambridge and King's Lynn line, while main line passenger trains from Liverpool Street to Norwich used the letter N, and S was allocated to trains running through Broxbourne to Bishop's Stortford. T was used for the Chingford line and U for the Enfield line. The letter X was especially reserved for Royal trains, while the letter Z was used for special charter trains.

The last two digits in this headcode system were simply a train identifier, as shown in the Working Timetable, and ran consecutively from 0 at midnight each day for each route, even numbers being used for Up trains and odd numbers for Down trains. It was part of the drivers' assistant's job to set these headcodes, winding the roller blinds provided in the indicator boxes on the front of the locomotives. These blinds eventually became too expensive to maintain, so after 1976 they were taken out of use and set to 0000, and in due course blanked off and replaced with marker lights. The two codes I became very familiar with were 0H01, which denoted light engine to Stratford, and 5H04, which was used for empty coaching stock from Liverpool Street to Thornton Fields carriage sidings near Stratford.

A different type of train identification inherited from the steam days, using lights and discs, could be found on some of the older locomotives, such as the early type 2s and type 4s. The classification for 3 and 4 trains were the same and in the end, class three was rarely used. This classification was for parcel trains and trains carrying perishable commodities, where the train was composed entirely of vehicles that conformed to coaching stock requirements. Other regions, such as the Southern and the Western, had different train reporting systems. The arrangement of those used on the Eastern Region, as I remember them, is shown below.

My first trips out on the road as a driver's assistant were to be fairly local. Signing on for duty early one morning, I checked the job allocated to the driver and me. We were to take an engine from the depot to Temple Mills, then work a freight train to a place called Channelsea. I remember thinking that it sounded like a place on the coast somewhere, but in actual fact it was, quite literally, just around the corner from the depot. What a let down! These sorts of 'trip' workings were very common,

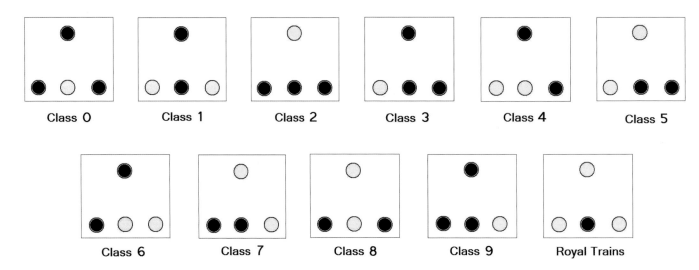

The configuration of lights used on the front of certain locomotives for train identification.

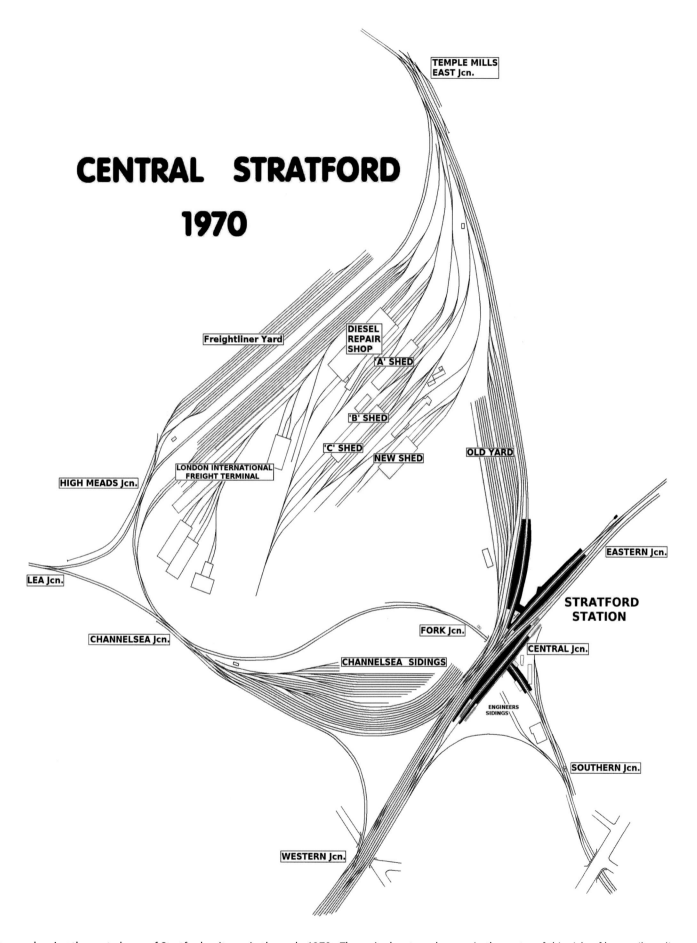

CENTRAL STRATFORD
1970

TEMPLE MILLS
EAST Jcn.

Freightliner Yard

DIESEL
REPAIR
SHOP

'A' SHED

'B' SHED

'C' SHED

NEW SHED

OLD YARD

LONDON INTERNATIONAL
FREIGHT TERMINAL

HIGH MEADS Jcn.

EASTERN Jcn.

LEA Jcn.

STRATFORD
STATION

CHANNELSEA Jcn.

FORK Jcn.

CENTRAL Jcn.

CHANNELSEA SIDINGS

ENGINEERS
SIDINGS

SOUTHERN Jcn.

WESTERN Jcn.

A map showing the central area of Stratford as it was in the early 1970s. The main depot can be seen in the centre of this cicle of busy railway lines. What can be seen on this map is a former shadow of what once occupied this area. Who would have thought that the once-mighty Stratford shed would eventually be razed to the ground to make way for the extension of the Channel Tunnel Rail Link in 2006.

Fork Junction signal box at Stratford. A busy place in the steam days, this box was relegated to shunting the North Woolwich DMUs into a turn-round siding whilst drivers had their meal breaks. Note the semaphore distant signal on the bracket-post near the bridge. This signal was related to the platform starting signal at Stratford Low Level station, the platform of which can be seen just through the bridge.

as there were a number of smaller goods yards dotted about the area that needed wagons transferred between them. Whilst I was still at the bottom of the proverbial career ladder, a lot of the jobs consisted of rather menial freight shunting work. This utilised small locomotives that were known as '350s', a direct reflection on the loco's horsepower. They later became known as the 08 and 09 Class, and although small in size, they were quite powerful. They were unusual in that they resembled steam locomotives, complete with large driving wheels and side rods!

We were allocated one of these locos one dark, foggy, morning to work a freight from Temple Mills to Silvertown, on the River Thames near North Woolwich. Once there, we were to shunt the various sidings for most of the morning in relation to large warehouses, such as Tate & Lyle sugar and Crosse & Blackwell. The '350s' had a wheel arrangement of 0-6-0 and were limited to a maximum speed of 20 miles per hour, and at this speed were very rough riding. Our job to Silvertown involved diving into a tunnel at Custom House to pass under the Victoria and Albert Docks on the Thames. At Custom House, the double line split into two single lines, one for passenger trains on the left, the other for freight trains on the right. Before we entered these lines, a metal token had to be picked up at the Custom House signal box to allow us onto the correct line. Once this was in our possession, we trundled down the incline into the murkiness of the tunnel. The weight of the train meant that we soon picked up speed, nudging the 20mph limit and a bit more. Suddenly, a large pillar of stone loomed out of the darkness. The train lurched to the right of this pillar and the driver whipped open the power controller! Was he mad?? It was at this point that the gradient started to rise, so if he hadn't took full power we would have stalled within the tunnel. What a frightening first experience!

At weekends, a lot of freight work consisted of working engineers' trains. These were either stone trains, used in association with track relaying, or special wiring trains that were sent out to renew some of the overhead electric power supply cables. This was also something new to me; overhead electric power. The voltages in the 1970s varied between 6,000 volts within the immediate London area, to 25,000 volts elsewhere. In later years, the system within the London area was changed, making the voltage 25,000 volts throughout. Whilst carrying

An unidentified '350' shunting locomotive has come to grief in the Thornton Fields carriage sidings, near Stratford, after derailing on a set of points, bending the side rods.

I am seen here, at this stage still a cleaner, leaning out of the cab of English Electric Type 3 number 6742 parked outside the 'B' Shed at Stratford Depot in 1970. These locos were soon to become known as Class 37s, and this loco would become 37 042. Note the green liveried Brush Type 2 in the background, numbered 5851.

A Brush Type 2 locomotive shows the disc and lights arrangement used for train identification, in this case showing a Class 7 configuration. These particular locos were nick-named 'toffee-apples' due to the shape of the power controller. This loco, number 5500, is seen standing in Tilbury Riverside yard with me in the doorway, and driver Joe Joseph at the controls. The train originally worked was the 14:00 from Temple Mills. The red dots above the buffers were related to the type of power control in use, in this case electro-magnetic. In later years, the locomotive became part of the National Railway Museum collection.

An overall view of Stratford depot in the 1970s, taken from the old water tower. Various classes of locomotives can be seen, ranging from 15s, 31s, 37s and a 47 in B shed.

out duties beneath these electrified wires, one always had to be very cautious not to get too close to the wires concerned, especially if using long-handled instruments for cleaning cab windows. We were informed that the safe working proximity was no less than three feet. Most of the traction units had an orange line painted around the ceiling height as an additional reminder as to the safe working limits. Ex-Stratford driver Reg Rowe was one of the few people to have survived having come into contact with live overhead equipment. He was in the tender

A sign that was literally plastered everywhere on the electrified lines of British Rail, to remind staff and the public of the dangers of coming too close to live overhead wires.

of his steam locomotive, attempting to drag some coal further down, when he was electrocuted; a simple act of forgetting that the wires were there.

A lot of things started to happen in 1971. On the home front, my parents found a property in a village called Elsenham, six miles north of Bishop's Stortford. This meant another house move, but would give us all permanent accommodation instead of lodging with our relatives. As I could not afford to rent a property of my own at this stage, I had no choice but to move with them. This played havoc with my travel arrangements at first, but luckily there was a railway station at Elsenham that had a direct service with Liverpool Street. Soon after this move, I was able to buy myself a small Honda 175 motorcycle to enable me to get to work on shifts when there was no train service. There were two choices; cycle to Epping, then either catch the Central Line, or use the bike to travel all the way to Stratford.

A lot of the mundane work carried out on shed at Stratford was preparation and disposal duties. This involved either getting locomotives ready for service, or fuelling and watering locomotives that had returned to the shed after completing their turn of duty for the day. This was known simply as P&D duty, and more often than not, gave the fireman a chance to drive the locomotives from the fuelling point to the shed, or positioned on the lines adjacent to the B and C shed. These lines were known as the 'steam roads', of which there were three.

A type of locomotive that was small but quite versatile was the British-Thompson-Houston Bo-Bo locomotives that became known as the Class 15s or 'BTHs' for short. They were colloquially known as the '82 hundreds', due to their numbering range. These locos were of a hood design that had the cab set back from one end, similar to the Australian 830-class. The engine used was a Paxman 16YHXL type, developing 800 horsepower. At weekends, they could be found on lightweight engineering trains such as utilised by the Overhead Line department, when renewing or repairing the overhead line equipment.

Also in 1971, the railways started to introduce a computerised freight information system. This was known as the Total Operations Processing System, or TOPS for short. It proved so popular that it was extended to cover the movements and control of locomotives and carriages. Previously, on the Eastern Region, this information was transmitted by telegraph, teleprinters and Telex. To suit this system of working, locomotive numbers had to consist of five numbers, so the original 'types' were broken down into 'classes'. The locomotives that I was associated with were changed as shown in the table below:-

Original number range	Type & Year built	TOPS Classification	Weight	Engine used
2200 - 2340	Type 1 1957	Class 04	31 tons	Gardner 8L3
3000 - 4192	Type 1 1957	Class 08	49 tons	English Electric 6KT
8200 - 8243	Type 1 1957	Class 15	68 tons	Paxman 16YHXL *
8000 - 8199	Type 2 1960	Class 20	72 tons	English Electric 8SVT
5500 -5699	Type 2 1957	Class 31	103 tons	English Electric 12SVT #
700 - 6999	Type 3 1960	Class 37	105 tons	English Electric 12CSVT
200 - 399	Type 4 1958	Class 40	133 tons	English Electric 16SVT
1100 - 1999	Type 4 1962	Class 47	123 tons	Brush Sulzer 12LDA28C
400 - 449	Type 4 1967	Class 50	115 tons	English Electric 16CSVT

* Locomotives 8234 and 8242 were kept for the Liverpool Street shunting locos when the rest of the class were scrapped in 1981.
\# Early Type 2s in the 5500 - 5520 range, had Mirrlees JVS12T engines rated at 1,250hp.

The 'Types' of locomotives were denoted according to their power output and were classified as follows:-
• Type 1 = up to 1,000 horsepower
• Type 2 = 1,001 to 1,500 hp
• Type 3 = 1,501 to 1,999 hp
• Type 4 = 2,000 to 2,999 hp
• Type 5 = 3,000 and above

A forlorn looking 6718 stands on the fuelling point at Stratford depot, after bringing the 09:27 from King's Lynn to Liverpool Street in 1971.

Two misty early morning views of BTH Class 15 locomotives, during weekend engineering
work on the overhead power lines between West Horndon and Laindon on the London
Tilbury and Southend line during the early 1970s. Note the engineers on the roof of the
wiring train. Number 8221 is seen below, where the above photograph was taken from.

Details of a BTH Class 15 locomotive, in this case number 8207, which was still in green livery. Note the 30A shed sticker on the left, and the steam-age British Railways transfer.

An unidentified BTH general purpose Class 15 locomotive is seen here manoeuvring the Stratford breakdown crane out of its New Shed home in 1971.

Another very common locomotive that I became familiar with were the Brush Type 2s that eventually became the Class 31s. The locomotives in the number range 5500 to 5519 were known as 'Toffee Apples' due to the unusual shape of the power controller. This handle was literally a ball on a stick, and was the master key that was rotated within its housing to put the locomotive into forward, reverse, neutral, or 'engine start'. To make the locomotive move forward, this control handle had to be carefully rotated to the 'forward' position, then pushed forward to increase the power and pulled back to decrease the power. They had a nasty habit of jamming in some positions, especially if the driver was a bit heavy-handed. These locomotives came with the light and disc arrangement on the front for train identification purposes, but from 5520 onwards, the new four character headcode boxes were fitted above the front windows.

It will be seen from some of the photos of these machines, that there used to be a gangway door fitted on the front of the Class 31s, but they were eventually sealed up. Internally, where this door used to be, there was an 8" deep housing that gave a handy shelf just below the central small front window. This shelf, more often than not, was used for placing the tea can. The suspension on the 31s was quite bouncy at speeds about 40 mph, and juddered quite a lot above this speed. One night, we were trundling along at a steady pace with one of these machines, when there was an almighty crashing noise within the cab. The driver switched on the light, to find the contents of the tea can strewn all over the floor! The can had vibrated itself off the shelf with all of the bouncy motion of the locomotive.

While I was at Stratford in the early 1970s, the 'Toffee Apple' Class 31s never strayed further than the old Great Eastern area and could be found working a variety of trains, including occasional trips on Cambridge passenger trains. This was usually when other motive power wasn't available. As a driver once said to me, "They couldn't pull the skin off a rice pudding." I tended to agree, as they took ages to reach any high speed above sixty miles per hour. Even with the later 31s, if they were ever used on a Norwich express, they were double-headed. They were more at home on goods trains such as the Hertford goods or the Bishop's Stortford goods, which incorporated the

A cab view of the early Class 31s that were known as 'Toffee Apples'. The control handle where this name was derived can be seen on the right. Note the old vacuum automatic brake valve handle on the left. Note also the hap-hazard way of curing draughts around the cab, by use of black tape!

odd trip to the Geest banana factory at Easton Lodge on the old Dunmow line. This line originally went through to Witham, *via* Braintree, but was closed between Easton Lodge and Braintree in 1969. The line from Bishop's Stortford to the banana factory eventually closed as well in February 1979, and the banana traffic was dealt with at Bishop's Stortford station for a short time, usually only one wagon a week being met by a road vehicle. Bishop's Stortford was still a busy place in the 1970s, having household coal delivered to the Down yard there as well as being an Electric Multiple Unit depot. The Up sidings were capable of stabling up to eight four-car units.

An interesting portrait of the different Brush Type 2 front ends, showing the two kinds of Train Identification in use. Note that the locomotive on the right, number 5661, has blue stars above the buffers, meaning that the power control on this loco was of the electro-pneumatic kind. Note also that 5500 had been through the works for a repaint and has had the number moved under the cab window. Compare this with the picture on page 51.

I had worked on the Hertford goods on quite a few occasions. This train conveyed a variety of commodities, ranging from household coal, which was left at the Broxbourne yard, and bitumen tanks that went through to Hertford East. Once the train reached Hertford, the tanks were shunted across Mead Lane into Pintar's private sidings, and the locomotive returned to its train for the trip back towards Broxbourne. On the way, it called in at Austin's siding at St. Margarets station to swap wagons from the maltings. This kind of industry was prevalent in this area, feeding the McMullen's brewery at Hertford. The train then headed towards Rye House to pick up loaded concrete sleeper wagons from the siding at Costains, closely following an electric passenger service due to the time it took to shunt single wagons at the concrete sleeper siding. Due to the very short shunting spur, only one wagon at a time could be shunted in and out of Costains siding and this took up quite a bit of time. (The spur was eventually lengthened in later years, but the siding closed in 1991). After the shunting had been completed here, the train went on to Broxbourne to pick up the empty coal wagons, before returning to Temple Mills.

Local trips from Temple Mills that utilised the Class 31s were runs to Poplar and East India Docks on the River Thames. These involved taking the train to Victoria Park in Hackney, then running around the train for the trip to Poplar. This meant that there was usually a brake van at each end of the train. This area was not the most salubrious of places, and even the guards were known to hide on the floor of their brakevans because of children throwing bricks at them! This particular line is now the home for London's Docklands Light Railway.

The 31s were no strangers to the London, Tilbury and Southend Railway (known as the LTS), and Stratford men had many jobs there. These ranged from pick-up goods trains to Tilbury Riverside, Freightliner container trains to the terminal at Tilbury, oil and petrol tank trains from the huge storage facility at Thames Haven, car trains from the massive Ford Motor car assembly plant at Dagenham Dock, and the afternoon parcel train to Southend Central. It was whilst we were working one of the pick-up goods with a 'Toffee Apple' 31 one foggy night that disaster nearly struck. We had left Temple

Mills and headed to Pitsea to run round the train. This enabled us to shunt sidings at Laindon, West Horndon and coal sidings between Becontree and Upney on the line that ran parallel to the District Line. It was while we were kicking off some loaded coal wagons to exchange for empties at this last siding that the fun began. Sid Woolnough was the driver for this trip, and he was known as a bit of a joker. He would always have the mess room in stitches with his antics. On this occasion, the shunter had required some loose shunting to be done, and in my opinion this was not a good choice, considering the dark, foggy weather. Sid duly twisted the 'Toffee Apple' into reverse, and shoved the controller forward to gain some momentum to knock about three loaded wagons off behind us. When the shunter unhooked these wagons and gave the hand signal to stop, Sid started to struggle with the controller to bring it back to the off position. I thought he was larking about as usual, until he slapped the automatic brake into emergency to cut off the power. This action was followed by an almighty crashing sound as the coal wagons had hit stationary wagons in the fog. We both jumped down to survey the damage, expecting wagons and coal to be lying all over the place, only to find that they had just made a heavy contact with each other.

When Sid was about Stratford depot, there was never a dull moment. One Christmas, he asked the foreman, Bill McMeakin, whether he could put up a few Christmas chains to brighten the mess room up a bit. Bill peered over his glasses and warily gave his consent. With this, Sid went out and dragged in some huge metal chains from the yard outside! The foreman was not amused.

Another class of locomotive that I became at home with was the English Electric Type 3s that became known as the Class 37s. These locomotives had a nose at both ends, which made turning the locomotive at the end of a journey a thing of the past. The Class 37s had a V12 engine in the 1,750hp range and, to me, sounded just like the 800-class locos I used to work with in Australia. The 37s were versatile locomotives which were at home on freight and passenger trains. One of my first experiences on these locos was working the sand train to and from Southminster.

We would take the empty sand hoppers to Southminster, a

The morning Hertford goods, with 'Toffee Apple' 5503 in charge, pauses in Austin's siding for the maltings at St. Margarets station on its way up to Broxbourne. The maltings buildings behind the train have since been converted to flats. Whilst at these sidings, I managed to pick some apples from a small orchard that sat to the right of the picture.

Locomotive 5512 sits in Poplar yard ready to leave with 9H56, the 12:15 to Temple Mills. We had originally brought in some wagons loaded with steel for the local docks on the Thames. This site is now dominated by the A1261 flyover and the Docklands Light Railway depot.

An empty sand train prepares to leave the sidings at Mile End, East London, with 6725 in charge. 8D20 was the 09:58 train for Southminster, off the Southend line, and would arrive at 12:05. After shunting the yard there we would return with 8H37, the 13:30 loaded train for Mile End. Note that the old nose gangway doors, which were rarely used, have been plated over.

branch line terminus off the Southend line, and then take loaded wagons back to Mile End in east London. This train had special instructions for running between Shenfield and Gidea Park, in that it was not to exceed 15 miles per hour before descending the incline at Brentwood. This was due to the steep falling gradient at this point, and the weight of the train. Watching this train running down this gradient with the brakes full-on was quite spectacular, with sparks coming off the brake blocks putting most Catherine-wheel fireworks to shame.

Apart from keeping a locomotive's cab spick and span with the aid of a dust-pan and brush, part of the driver's assistant's job was to attend to the carriage heating equipment on locomotives, that was officially known as a steam generator. This was something else that was a new experience for me, as I was used to carriages that either had air-conditioning as standard, or were heated with foot warmers. The steam generators, or boilers as we called them, produced steam that was piped through the train to under-seat radiators. If we ran a light engine to London for a passenger working, it was the assistant's job to make sure the boiler was in good working order, and that there was plenty of water. On arrival in London, once the locomotive was squeezed against the carriages, it was then the assistant's job to couple up to the train using the 70lb screw coupling. This was no mean feat from a crouching position between loco and train, but luckily my small stature was on my side. With practice, I was soon able to jump down between the loco and train, throw the coupling on, connect up the brake and steam pipes, and be out again before the driver could blink. Care had to be taken when uncoupling in the winter, as the steam pipe connections could still be scalding hot, even though the boiler was shut down about four miles before arriving at Liverpool Street. I was doing this very job on a Class 37 with an Up Norwich express one day, when the driver opened up the throttle after slowing for a speed restriction and one of the turbo blowers blew up! It was the quickest I have ever left an engine room.

The picture above right shows what the driver's assistant or guard had to become familiar with, to be able to couple two locomotives together, or couple a locomotive to a train. The first rule of thumb was to get the locomotive squeezed up to the vehicle concerned, and then throw the coupling onto the vehicle's hook. On passenger trains, this had to be screwed

The buffer beam arrangements of a Class 31 locomotive. The numbered components are as follows: 1, Jumper cable socket; 2, Control air pipe; 3, Main reservoir air pipe; 4, Vacuum brake pipe; 5, Screw coupling; 6, Steam heating pipe; 7, Multiple-working jumper cable; 8, Air brake pipe; 9, AWS receiver.

up as tight as possible to prevent the coaches lurching about when power was taken at the controller. Once the assistant was happy with this, he usually signalled to the driver to ease away from the train to allow more space for coupling all the relevant pipes.

The first priority was to release the vacuum pipe from the locomotive, to prevent any further movement by the driver whilst there was someone between the loco and train. To do this, the driver had to place the automatic brake valve to emergency to destroy the vacuum within the brake pipe, otherwise it was nearly impossible to get the pipe away from its dummy mounting. The steam pipes were then connected together (winter only), followed

Class 42 'Warship' diesel-hydraulic locomotive number 818, named *Glory*, at Kensington Olympia, prepares to take the Ilford milk train back to Devon after exchanging locomotives. This loco was based at Newton Abbot Depot (83A).

A picture taken at an unusual angle of the dwarf ground signal and associated disc shunting signal at the Ilford milk processing and bottling depot. The six-wheeled milk tanks can just be seen on the left.

by the vacuum pipes. In later years, air brakes were introduced to passenger services, and this meant that there were also a main-reservoir and brake pipes to connect instead of the vacuum pipe.

I was slowly making my way up though the links, venturing further afield with each link promotion. I had some interesting jobs to the Western Region, to places like Reading, and the Southern Region to places like the Bricklayers Arms freight depot (no longer in existence) near London Bridge, Clapham Junction, West Norwood and Hither Green. Sometimes on these inter-regional workings, we only went as far as Kensington Olympia, and each locomotive swapped trains. This was the case with the Ilford milk train. The train that originated from Devon, would roll in with a Western Region 'Warship' locomotive and a string of six-wheeled milk tanks, for instance, and we would then couple-up our Class 37 and take the train forward to the processing plant at Ilford in east London. This had its benefits, as we were allowed to have some free samples from the production line, and I used to opt for the chocolate milk shakes! Alas, this place no longer exists either. Sometimes at Kensington, we would change locomotives with oil trains that had come from Micheldever on the Southern region or Thame in Oxfordshire, and then take them onwards to either Ripple Lane marshalling yard, Purfleet, or the Thames Haven refinery.

Not all of my duties as a driver's assistant at this stage involved freight work. Sometimes empty coaching stock work was thrown in for good measure; at least it broke the monotony of long drags from Temple Mills to Whitemoor, between Ely and Peterborough. On one of these freight trains, I remember that we had to take a Class 08 shunter that had had its side rods

One of the two signal boxes at Kensington Olympia that controlled the mix of lower and upper quadrant signals at this location. The other box was called Kensington North Main.

taken off, from Temple Mills to Whitemoor. That was all very well, but our speed was restricted to 25 mph and the 85 mile journey took over four hours due to the regular stops having to be made to check the shunting loco.

Most of my favourite jobs were working the hauled passenger trains to and from King's Lynn. The job usually ran something like this; light engine from Stratford to Liverpool Street, hook up to the appropriate train, and off to King's Lynn. On arrival there, the driver's assistant unhooked the loco which then ran round the

train, and hooked onto the London end. There was about an hour allocated for this purpose. The train was then worked back to London, where the job came to an end. During the hour at King's Lynn, some drivers used to visit the town's market to purchase fresh sausages (which, oddly enough, came from London in the first place). Rail staff at King's Lynn also had some perks from the Campbell's soup factory that was just around the corner from the station. We were able to purchase cans of soup at five pence per can, but due to the greediness of a few, this perk came to an end.

A trainload of fuel oil tanks from the Southern region arrives at Kensington Olympia with electro-diesel number E6010 at the head (above). Note the drop-down automatic (Buckeye) coupling hanging from the draw hook. This would have been used when the locomotive worked passenger trains. Whilst I was a driver's assistant, the Eastern region never adopted these couplings on locomotives. The train is 6E38, destined for Ripple Lane and, eventually, the Thames Haven refinery. This loco's home depot was south London's Stewarts Lane (75D).

The locomotive rostered for working 6E38 was usually a Type 3, and here we see 6727 about to depart Kensington Olympia with the 100-ton tanks just brought in by the electro-diesel seen in the previous picture.

I am pictured here as a secondman, posing in the doorway of a two-tone green Type 4 locomotive at Kensington Olympia. This was unusual motive power for 6E38, which was usually rostered a Type 3

An afternoon line-up of English Electric Type 3s in Thornton Fields carriage sidings, waiting to work empty coaching stock into Liverpool Street. I was working the train on the left, 5K62 with 6725, which formed the empties for the 16:56 to Ipswich *via* Cambridge. The train in the centre was 5L28, which made the 18:22 service to Cambridge, while the train on the right, 5L22, was the empties for the 17:16 Cambridge.

Some views while working cross-London freight trains could be very interesting. The above 1970s vista is the view from the North London Line, overlooking King's Cross and St. Pancras stations. The smoke emanating from Gasworks Tunnel suggests that a 'Deltic' locomotive had just departed the London terminal. The tracks on the right led into King's Cross goods yard. This scene has now totally changed due to the introduction of the Channel Tunnel Rail Link into St. Pancras station.

The misty scene at north London's Cricklewood Brent Empty sidings on the Midland Region. The sidings here were very tightly spaced, and there was not a lot of room to walk between them. Note the very basic hut that controlled the movements in and out of the yard. The one in the foreground has been replaced by another one that is not much larger, after suffering fire damage.

Two views of the same locomotive, but in different liveries before the TOPS numbering system was introduced. Above, a green 6817 is seen in platform ten at Liverpool Street with empty coaches for Thornton Fields carriage sidings, whilst below, she is seen in ex-works condition after receiving the all-over corporate blue livery, waiting to work the 11:20 parcels to Romford. The train ran-round at Gidea Park and returned to Channelsea sidings, calling at Ilford on the way. I worked both trains as a secondman.

A busy week-day scene at London's Liverpool Street station in the early 1970s, with a variety of locomotives in evidence. A Type 3 stands in the loco holding sidings, while a green Type 2 stands in platform 10 waiting to work empties to Thornton Fields. In platform 9, a two-tone green Type 4 waits to work the 10:30 Norwich express, with a freshly painted 6817 standing in platform 8 with the 11:20 parcels train for Romford.

A busy Saturday scene at the end of platform 10 at Liverpool Street, with the trainspotters out in force. Notice the tight confines of the holding sidings, with no less than four locomotives in evidence.

The 15:34 Up stopping service from Cambridge is seen leaving Stansted station in the mid 1970s, with 6727 hauling Mk.1 coaching stock. This station was later named Stansted Mountfitchet to save confusion with Stansted Airport when a railway service was built there in 1990. Note the semaphore signal just above the second coach, and the signal box which can just be seen behind the sixth coach. The hill in the background was the site used for the rebuilding of Mountfitchet Castle, which purported to date from 1066.

Photo: Brian R. Bandt / R. Taylor collection

Another Up Cambridge service is seen between Newport and Elsenham station, this time with Mk.2 coaching stock. Note also that the headcode indicators had by this stage been changed to two white dots.

CHAPTER V
Top Link

As time progressed, I began to work more express services to and from Norwich, and was put in link sixteen, considered the top link, in June of 1974. Most of the time, the motive power used was the Brush Type 4, later known as the Class 47s, although Class 37s deputised on the odd occasion. On one such occasion during the summer, we had one of the Class 37s on the outward trip to Norwich. We had slowed down in the Mellis area for a 20mph speed restriction, but could not find the termination board that ended the restriction. The next minute, the fire alarm bell started to ring. It was my job to investigate, and when I entered the engine room, I could see the problem. Because we had been travelling at only 20mph for quite a distance, there had been no rush of cooling air through the radiator fan, and the exhaust manifold above the engine was literally glowing red-hot! Needless to say, the locomotive was changed upon our arrival at Norwich.

One of the most interesting jobs in this link was the one where we worked the 19:30 departure from Liverpool Street to Norwich, then returned with the 23:15 mail train that ran *via* Cambridge. This train reached Brandon at about midnight, and left Cambridge at 01:00. As this particular route crossed the fenland area of East Anglia, our journey was often made in thick fog. Bearing in mind that the locos in those days never had any headlights, the trip from Norwich to Cambridge on this train was always done in pitch darkness. A driver certainly had to know the 'road' along this stretch, where numerous semaphore signals still existed, complete with dim kerosene lamps. Usually, a driver could take his bearings from audible landmarks, such as river bridges or level crossings.

Quite often on these jobs, because the driver's assistant was an experienced man by this stage in his career, the driver often gave him the choice of having a drive. The deal was usually "You take it down and I'll bring it back." Although this was not an officially recognised practice, from my experience in Australia, it would seem that it was a very common occurrence around the world. Most of the time, the assistant was under the instruction of the driver. In reality, it was really the only way of gaining the practical experience required to become a driver. One particular evening, I had been allowed to drive the 19:30 train from Liverpool Street to Norwich under instruction, and the driver was going to take the train back to London, *via* Cambridge. The trouble was, taking advantage of my experience, the driver had too much liquid refreshment in a nearby establishment during the break at Norwich, so I was obliged to take the train back to London as well. What made the situation worse, was the fact he came weaving down the platform towards the locomotive at the very minute the platform staff were blowing the whistle to give me the 'right-away'! It was certainly a test of my route knowledge from Norwich to Cambridge in the dark!

These kinds of practices were a throw-back to the days of steam, when the train crews were under the impression that they were able to sweat off any effects of alcohol. There were systems in place to guard against such practices, whereby crews were supposed to report such instances. These systems were flawed in that they didn't take into account the loyalty (misguided as it was) between footplatemen. Rules have been extremely tightened since those days, and as well as being a criminal offence, any member of staff is now liable to dismissal if they appear for duty under the influence of drugs or alcohol, or consumes such whilst on duty. And quite rightly so.

After working the mail train from Norwich, we ended up back at Stratford at about 02:12 the next morning. The only way I could get home from this job was to hitch a lift from Stratford on the loco that worked the 04:00 newspaper train from London to Cambridge, and get off at Bishop's Stortford if my motorcycle was left there, or get dropped off at Elsenham by the obliging train crew. Some other jobs finished about 00:30, and at one stage, I was able to hitch a lift on the Leeds Freightliner train which left the Stratford terminal at about 01:00 in the morning. Once or twice, this train was worked by an English Electric Type 4 (Class 40) which was a way of returning the locomotive back to the Leeds district after the loco had had its wheels turned on the Stratford wheel lathe.

Some of the jobs were quite drawn out and I was away from home for quite a long time. It was a case of get up, go to work, come home, and go straight to bed ready for the next turn of duty. On these occasions, there was no social life at all. One case in point was the afternoon trip to Ipswich, *via* Cambridge and Bury St. Edmunds, which was colloquially called the 'Bury round', as we literally completed a round trip. We signed on about 15:15 and travelled to London to work our first train. This was the 16:08 departure to Cambridge, which we took on to Ipswich and then had a break. We then worked a train just after 22:00 which arrived in London at 23:45. For this particular job, I had to catch the 13:40 railcar from Elsenham and change at Bishop's Stortford for the fast hauled connection for Liverpool Street. I then had to make my way to Stratford to sign on. By the time we finished at 23:45, the last train had left, so I had to hang around for the 04:00 paper train (carrying newspapers and associated staff) which got me back home by about 05:30 in the morning. It was then a matter of going straight to bed so I could get up again at around midday for my next afternoon shift.

It was difficult not to forget my first trip over the Bury St. Edmunds line as a second man. The job entailed relieving the driver of the 04:30 passenger train from Liverpool Street at Stratford at 04:40 in the morning, then taking this train as far as Ipswich. We then had about twenty minutes for a cup of tea before working the 07:05 train, 1K29, from Ipswich to London *via* Cambridge. This involved working along the single line from Chippenham Junction to Newmarket through a very narrow tunnel. This particular stretch of line was worked under a single-line token system of working, similar to the Electric Staff working that I was familiar with in Australia. On this first trip, as I leaned out of the cab door to retrieve the token from the Chippenham signalman, my hat flew off!

Having no time to stop and collect my hat, I wrote it off as a lost cause. By pure luck, we had the same job the following day, and when I collected the token at Chippenham, the signalman was pointing to the top of his head and then pointing towards Newmarket. It all became clear as we came out of the tunnel and entered Newmarket station. There was the signalman with my hat, so we did a quick swap, hat for token!

When hauled trains were worked into Liverpool Street and the locomotive was uncoupled, the crews were sometimes required to wait on the loco which was then used to work another train out of the London terminus. Whilst waiting on the locomotive at

> 'The driver had too much liquid refreshment in a nearby establishment during the break at Norwich, so I was obliged to take the train back to London'

Brush Type 4 number 1530 in two-tone green, sits at Liverpool Street waiting to work the 09:30 express to Norwich. The driver, wearing a summer-issue lightweight blue denim jacket, can just be seen through the cab window.

A cab view from the driver's assistant's seat of a Class 47 locomotive, taken at Norwich Thorpe station in the mid 1970s, a view not enhanced by the grotty state of the cab window!

the buffer-stop end of the station like this, we were able to share a joke or two with the travelling public. This was often hard work, as the great British commuter sometimes lacked a sense of humour. Take for instance the public's query of "How long is the next train?" When given the reply "About four coaches mate." we were often met with a blank look. Another question I have heard drivers give a teasing answer to was "Are you going to Cambridge?" The driver, quite rightly, had answered "No," and after a slight pause, "But that train that we are not hooked up to is."

The hauled passenger work at Stratford was quite varied, and ranged from the Cambridge and King's Lynn services, to Norwich expresses and Harwich boat trains. The boat trains were non-stop trains that were run in conjunction with the sailings of certain ferry services to the Hook of Holland or Esbjerg. Sometimes we were rostered to work a Freightliner train to Parkeston Quay, leaving Stratford at 02:20 in the morning, then, after a short break at Parkeston, work the 'European', a passenger train that went as far as Manchester. It was our job to take this train as far as Ipswich, and then work the 08:48 passenger to London.

Another class of locomotive in the Type 4 bracket that became my all-time favourite was the English Electric Class 40. They were commonly known as 'two thousands' by Stratford drivers, a reflection on their brake horsepower. They were equipped with the Mk.II version of that famous EE 16SVT engine, similar

to the version I was familiar with in the South Australian 900-class. The difference with the Class 40 was the maximum power output at 850 rpm instead of the Mk.I's 750 rpm, and this made a marked difference with the whistle that the turbo-chargers made; so much so that they became known as 'Whistlers' to railway enthusiasts. These locomotives made occasional visits to Stratford for certain repairs, or just for refuelling purposes. In 1959, three of these Type 4 locomotives were allocated to Stratford depot. These were locomotives D200, D202 and D203. The others of this early batch were allocated to Hornsey depot on the Great Northern main line.

The Class 40s, as they became known, were heavy machines weighing 133 tons. This made them nine tons heavier than their Australian 900-class counterparts, but this was probably due to the carriage heating apparatus and associated water tank. By the time I started at Stratford, these locomotives had been given homes elsewhere. It was a shame, as I would have loved to have regularly worked with them, but crews that were associated with them said they were very draughty to work with. That said, I did manage one official trip on one as an assistant, working light engine between Stratford and Ferme Park near Hornsey.

I liked these locos so much, that I eventually joined the Class Forty Preservation Society to help raise money for the preservation of D200 and D345. D345 eventually became 40 145, and became famous for being one of the first preserved locomotives to be capable of full main-line running. I have managed to travel on two excursions behind this preserved locomotive. The first trip was the 'Capital Whistler' tour from Crewe to King's Cross, the other was the 'Silver Jubilee' rail tour which I managed from Peterborough to Liverpool Street, then on to Norwich. On this trip, 40 145 managed to break the non-stop record set by D200 between London and Ipswich by 9½ minutes, completing that section in one hour and eight minutes. She completed the whole trip from London to Norwich in 104 minutes! Not bad for a preserved 40 year-old locomotive. The picture on page 125 shows the 'Silver Jubilee' train as it was passing through Elsenham station, on its way from Peterborough to Liverpool Street *via* Cambridge.

During the mid-1970s, British Rail introduced excursion trips called 'Merrymakers'. The idea was, for a flat fare of £5.00, you could board the train at a local station then travel to a destination that would not normally be available without having to change trains two or three times. I managed to travel on three of these tours.

One of these 'Merrymaker' trips from the Cambridge line took us to Newport in Monmouthshire, while another managed to reach Scarborough on the east coast. The Scarborough trip was interesting in that on the last leg of the journey, a Class 40 locomotive was used to replace the train locomotive at York. Most of the time on these excursions, the train crew would be changed several times due to lack of route knowledge for the entire trip. On one occasion, a 'Merrymaker' tour from Cambridge to Portsmouth Harbour, for the Isle of Wight, a Class 37 was used for the trip. The Stratford driver, Tony Gooding, ended up taking the train through to its destination because the Southern Region driver did not know how to drive Class 37s. He was therefore required to pilot the Stratford driver to Portsmouth.

During this part of my career, I was quite often using my latest acquisition, a 1951 BSA 'A10 Golden Flash', to get to and from work. In doing so, I obviously had to dress the part (especially in winter), and this meant a leather jacket and jeans. Being too lazy to change once I arrived at work, I would quite often carry out my duties as a 'secondman', as the assistant's job was now being called, wearing this garb. This came in handy when I needed to uncouple locomotives from trains, as grease was more easily removed from a leather jacket than it was from normal material.

During one Christmas period, there were special arrangements for drivers to get in to work. Due to the lack of an early train service on Boxing Day, a van was going to be provided to act as a taxi for those that needed it. As I lived over

English Electric Type 3 number 6749 stands at Parkeston Quay station while waiting to work the 17:35 boat train back to Liverpool Street in the mid 1970s. Note that there were only two operational arms on the semaphore bracket signal. The short arm took trains into the yard and the long arm applied towards the main line.

English Electric Type 4 number 345 stands in the holding sidings at King's Cross, waiting to work a passenger service to Newcastle-on-Tyne, a regular job for these locomotives in the 1970s. This locomotive was preserved by the Class Forty Preservation Society as 40 145, and was eventually capable of full main line running again.

A 1960's view of an English Electric Type 4, D253, standing outside the impressive Diesel Repair Shop at Stratford Depot. Note the small yellow warning panel and the ladder on the nose. This locomotive would have been visiting Stratford to have some mechanical attention, most probably wheel turning. JACK SEARLE/R TAYLOR COLLECTION

A 1970 publicity logo used in conjunction with a service from Finsbury Park to Newcastle that featured an image of a Class 40 locomotive. This was a set fare service (35/- or £1.75 in today's money) that used the Class 40 locomotives, and stopped at Potters Bar, Stevenage, Eaglescliffe, Stockton, Hartlepool, Sunderland and Newcastle-on-Tyne.

30 miles away, this wasn't going to be an option for me, so I was allowed to come in on the first available train. I hadn't relished the idea of using my motorbike during the freezing weather, and besides, I was not being paid a petrol allowance for using my own vehicle. When I arrived at Stratford to sign on for duty, I informed the running foreman that the circumstances would be the same for the rest of the week, due to the fact I had no early train that would suit my very early start. The foreman, not known for his tact and diplomacy, bellowed "What sort of game do you think you're playing? You know it's up to you to get yourself in for duty." The whole office fell into silence, and to cut a long story short, there was a verbal slanging match between him and me. In the end, I stated "Right, that's it. I'm off home!" The foreman stated "You can't do that!" and I retorted, "Watch me."

Needless to say I ended up on a charge of "Adopting a belligerent attitude and leaving the premises in a rage," and had to visit the depot master, Mr. Bill Lincoln, to explain my actions. I explained to him that, for some reason, I wasn't allowed to claim a petrol allowance for using my motorcycle and the offer of providing the company van as a taxi did not extend to Elsenham. I had no choice but to use the first available train. I also explained that the running foreman's attitude left a lot to be desired, what with his ranting and raving, and that it left me in such a state that I was unable to carry out my duties in a safe and responsible manner. Mr. Lincoln accepted what I had said, and promised to have a word with the foreman concerned. As I was reaching for the door handle, he called me back. "One more thing, about your manner of dress," referring to my wearing of a leather jacket to work. He explained that, as I was working on Norwich expresses and more in view of the travelling public, I ought to make an effort to wear the uniform provided. He was going to keep an eye on me in future, and if there were any further instances of going absent without leave, I would be re-appearing on his Axminster.

It was not long after this episode that I became a father (on

Stratford driver reaches Portsmouth Harbour! Tony Gooding poses for the camera with the signal box as a backdrop in 1977.

Father's Day!), with the birth of my son Barry in June 1975, so I really needed the promotion and the associated pay rise. My basic wage in 1975 was about £28.00 per week. To think that I had been on roughly £25.00 a week when I left Australia, it had taken me four years to reach the equivalent wage from my £8.00 cleaner's wage at Stratford! The beginning of 1976 came as a tough year for me. The lower age limit for driving trains on British Railways had been twenty-three for years, but in the very year that I was to turn twenty-three years of age, the age limit was lowered to twenty-one to help overcome a drastic shortage of drivers. February was lined up for me to take my initial rules exam, but it annoyed me that I could have been doing the exam two years previously. On the day of the exam, I had to appear at the main Hamilton House offices at Norton Folgate, situated adjacent to the east side of Liverpool

An admiring group of school children pause to speak to driver Tony Gooding after the marathon 'Merrymaker' trip from Cambridge to Portsmouth Harbour in 1977.

A picture of yours truly as a secondman, taken at Norwich by Stratford driver Bernie Brockbank (just to use up some of his film), whilst waiting to work an express back to Liverpool Street. With maturity, it is easy to see now why Depot Master Bill Lincoln took a dim view of my 'manner of dress'. DRIVER BERNIE BROCKBANK/R TAYLOR COLLECTION

ask a question of one man, then turn to another and ask, "Is he right?" In such a manner that it instantly cast doubt as to whether the original answer was correct. He would then give us a scenario involving an imaginary trip from 'A' to 'B' and throw in some awkward situations. These might involve operating or mechanical problems. When the scenario changed, Clem's favourite catch phrase was "Another day, another story." By the time lunchtime came around, I was sent home for not knowing enough to satisfy him. I had failed the exam miserably. Afterwards, Clem took me to one side and said that he was disappointed and had expected more from me. My failure to pass the exam was a wake-up call for me. I knew what the problem was, the same old story that had cropped up during my last year at school - homework! It was all very well being able to do the job in a practical sense, but a driver must know the Rule Book inside out for safety reasons. There had been Mutual Improvement Classes held voluntarily after work, but because of the distance I had to travel to get to work, I had never bothered to attend. My days were long enough already.

My exam failure had been a bitter pill to swallow, and what made it worse was the fact I now had a family to support, with a son who was seven months old. I desperately needed the promotion!

Street station. The corridors of this large building were quite intimidating, and I couldn't help thinking that it was all part of the psychological process to maintain the aura of knowing one's place in the railway hierarchy. It was typical of railway offices of the era, even down to the polished brown lino flooring that squeaked underfoot. Three other men were joining me for the same exam, and we were a bundle of nerves. Although many of us had good practical experience as railwaymen, the idea of the exam was for us to prove to the head Traction Inspector that we could interpret the rules in the 1950 version of the British Railways Rule Book. As with any exam, the questions were only difficult if you didn't know the answer!

Clem Britten was the man appointed to take our exam, and he started off with a few questions that seemed fairly easy to answer. Then the pace was stepped up a bit. He would

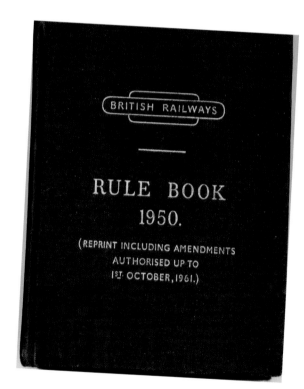

The cover of the British Railways Rule Book, 1950, the revised 1961 version.

The picture above shows the driver's controls of a Class 37 locomotive. These were very similar to Class 40 and 55 locomotives. They are as follows:- 1, independent brake valve; 2, window wiper control; 3, AWS cancelling button; 4, AWS indicator; 5, train's automatic brake valve (in shutdown position); 6, speedometer; 7, main generator ammeter; 8, driver's throttle handle; 9, engine start button; 10, reverser handle (in off position).

The controls on the driver's assistant's side of a Class 37 cab. They are as follows:- 1, door into the nose compartment; 2, boiler operating light; 3, loco horn; 4, boiler emergency shut-down button; 5, boiler steam pressure gauge; 6, water tank capacity; 7, handbrake wheel; 8, window wiper valve; 9, emergency fire extinguisher handle for engine-room.

A wet day ahead awaits a Cambridge service at Liverpool Street's platform 7 in the 1970s, above, with the impressive Primrose Street girder bridge dominating the picture.

The 12:36 service to King's Lynn is standing in platform 8 at Liverpool Street, but is carrying the wrong headcode which should read 1L24.

74

My regular driver in the 'Norwich gang' was Len Spill, seen here posing on platform 9 at Liverpool Street, with the infamous trip to Norwich in the summer when the overheated exhaust manifold set off the fire alarm.

My two eldest children, Barry and Anne, are seen here in this wintry scene at Elsenham station in approximately 1986 with an Up Cambridge service arriving in the charge of a Class 47 locomotive, a step up from the normal Class 37 haulage. My son eventually followed in my footsteps and became a train driver at Bishop's Stortford.

Unusual Visitors to Stratford.

Class 40 locomotives often visited Stratford after working Freightliner trains from the north, and came on shed to be refuelled. Here we see number 339 sitting adjacent to 'A' shed while waiting for its next turn of duty.

A locomotive that was powered by a similar English Electric V-16 engine as the Class 40s, was the Class 50. These locomotives were the first types to be originally fitted with dynamic brakes from new. One of the later refurbished types is also seen here alongside the DMU 'A' shed at Stratford.

A Class 46 locomotive sits outside the Diesel Repair Shop at Stratford after receiving attention on the wheel-turning lathe. As some of these locos were named after mountains, they were commonly referred to as 'Peaks'.

The cab layout of a class 46 locomotive. The numbered items are as follows: 1, Independent Brake Valve; 2, Automatic Brake Pipe Pressure; 3, Vacuum Gauge; 4, Brake Cylinder Pressure; 5, Speedometer; 6, Main Generator Ammmeter; 7, A.W.S Cancelling Button; 8, A.W.S Indicator; 9, Main Reservoir Pressure Gauge; 10, Power Handle; 11, Reverser Handle.

A Western Region Class 52 locomotive, number D1009, sits in east London's Manor Yard at Temple Mills in the 1970s. The Class 52s were commonly known as 'Westerns', and this particular loco had the name *Western Invader*, although it appears that the nameplates have been removed. This locomotive was based at Swansea's Landore Depot (87A). It was hauling was an articulated car-carrying train known as 'Cartics'.

Whilst I was a member of the Class Forty Preservation Society in 1983, I won an internal competition to design a new logo for the club, (commemorating the Class 40's 25 years of service), that could be used on stationery and 'T'-shirts. The result is reproduced above.

CHAPTER VI
In the Chair

The British Railways 1950 Rule Book was a complicated affair that even a solicitor would have had trouble interpreting. The version that I had to make myself conversant with was the reprinted and revised 1961 edition, but all this did was tidy up what would have been relevant to the steam era. The basics were still the same, with rule number one dealing with discipline. This stated that employees were to reside at a given location and turn up for duty at the appointed place and time. The idea of the rulebook was to provide a uniform set of instructions that railway staff were to adhere to for the general working of trains, and in times of disruption. This meant knowing what to do in the event of a breakdown or accident. The driver was supposed to be familiar with rules relating to other members of staff that his job was likely to bring him into contact with, which meant that he should know most of a signalman's and guard's duties as well as his own. Not only this, but he was to be totally conversant with the types of traction he was driving to enable him to carry out minor fault finding when things went wrong. This meant assimilating reams of paperwork relating to the job. People often thought it was an easy job to drive a train, and the physical side of it itself was easy if one knew what one was doing. It was when things went wrong that experience shone through.

After failing at my first attempt of the rules exam, about mid way through 1976 I was given another chance. I endured a further morning of 'Another day, another story' until the lunch break came around. Clem, in his usual manner, dismissed a couple of the contenders and sent them home. I was informed to take a break, and then if I could answer the afternoon's few questions successfully, I would be past the winning post. I'm afraid that nerves got the better of me, and I just could not think straight. I failed the exam again! This was getting serious, because I had one last chance and that would be it. It was a case of 'Three strikes and you're out'. If I failed for the third time, I would be looking for that job with the Merchant Navy and working my way back to Australia.

Towards the end of 1976, changes were made to what was known as the Promotion, Transfer and Redundancy rules, and a system known as MP12 was put in place. Just after this, I re-sat the rules exam for the third time and passed! This had a profound effect, because under the new MP12 arrangements, it was considered that I had sat the exam for the first time and was therefore entitled to have my driver's rate of pay backdated. This meant a payment of just over £1,000 was due to me, and as I was paid by cash, this was given to me in two instalments, along with my normal wages. It took me some time to count through the bundle of banknotes to ensure it was all there before rushing over to the bank in Stratford Broadway to deposit the money.

After this, things started to move in a positive direction. On the 14th February 1977, I began a training course on the Class 47 locomotives at the Ilford training school. Initially, the Class 37s were considered the basic locomotive that prospective drivers were to learn, and I had in fact started a course on the Type 3s in January 1976. As always, the railways moved the goal posts. After the first two poor attempts at my rules exams, I was determined to give a good impression. I finished this course on the 15th April, and by the end of it, I had produced a drawing of the side view and plan of the Class 47s that eventually was copied by the Ilford Training School and used as a teaching aid. My drawing of the Class 47 locomotive proved one thing, that I was better at applying myself at practical things rather than the theoretical elements. I could do all of the physical things required of me to carry out my duties, but I couldn't see the point of the 'whys and wherefores' except, of course, for safety reasons. I was the same at school with my mathematical studies. Who on earth needed to know about logarithms and Pythagoras' Theorem unless one was intending to become an engineer? I sat the exam for the Class 47s with inspector Tom Clancey, and he eventually ran out of questions to ask me. I knew everything there was to know about the locomotives. With the 47s, it turned out that not many of the class were identical with each other, with each one having minor differences in one way or another. One obvious difference was the braking systems, with some locos having Davies and Metcalfe, and others having the usual standard Westinghouse. Internally, some locos had a pre-start governor and others didn't. Some of the 47s were fitted with Spanner carriage heating equipment, while those on the Western had Stones boilers fitted.

> 'Who on earth needed to know about logarithms and Pythagoras' Theorem unless one was intending to become an engineer?'

The Class 47s, as the Brush Type 4s became known, were originally built in 1962 and were introduced to the ex-Great Eastern during 1964. When built, these locomotives had a horsepower rating of 2,750. The first locos of this class that were allocated to Stratford were numbers D1538, D1555, and D1565. Eventually, between October 1966 and January 1967, sixteen further units were transferred to Stratford from March depot. During the Queen's Silver Jubilee in 1977, two Class 47s were adorned with huge Union Jack flags painted on both sides; 47 163 appearing in June of that year, and 47 164 soon after.

After my initial training on the Class 47s, I eventually went on to learn quite a few more forms of traction. For ease of reference, I have compiled a table that shows all of the types I became familiar with and eventually drove, and this is shown on page 81. The basic traction unit was taught first, and then if the next form of traction was similar, this was known as a conversion course, and therefore did not take so long to learn. The initials EMU stood for Electric Multiple Unit, whilst DMU was short for Diesel Multiple Unit.

It was decided to name a train 'The Jubilee', and the 08:30 departure from Liverpool Street to Norwich was chosen for the Down working and the return 15:48 Up working from Norwich. A special headboard was constructed and used for these trains. Part of the training on the Class 47s involved practical handling for brake training experience, and this usually entailed a week on the Norwich expresses, as these were the trains that this class of locomotive was most often utilised. The 08:30 from Liverpool Street was usually chosen for the outward journey and the training was split into three parts, with the first trainee taking the train from Liverpool Street to Colchester, the next one taking the train from Colchester to Ipswich, and the final trainee taking the train for the final leg from Ipswich to Norwich. On the day of my practical exam, I had the privilege of taking the train on the first leg of the journey, and as I was already well practised at the job, the examining inspector and the trains' driver more or less chatted amongst themselves, leaving me to it!

Training on the brake handling on some of the locomotives involved working freight trains, and this meant sometimes

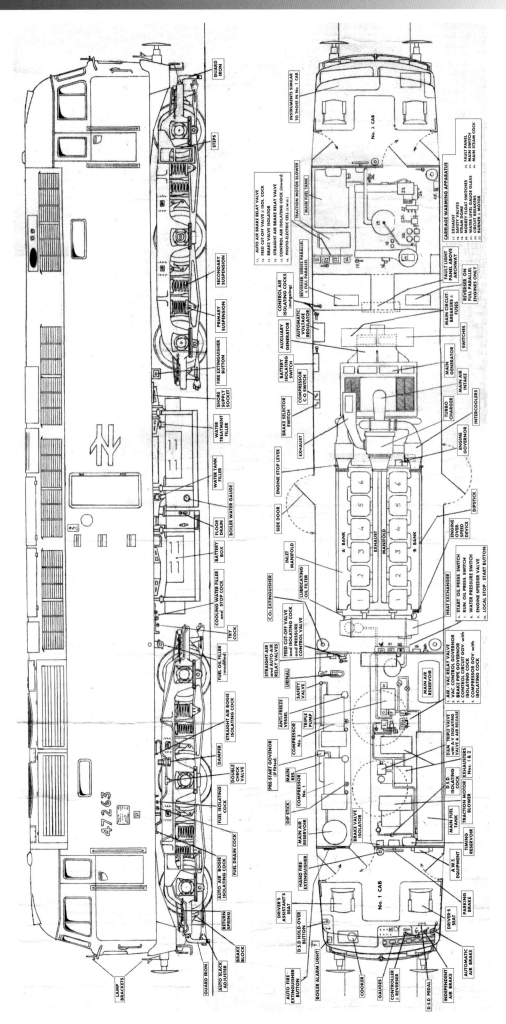

A reproduction of the original drawing that I drew with a ballpoint pen whilst on the training course for the Class 47 locomotives at the Ilford Training School. This drawing was eventually used as a teaching aid for other trainee drivers at the school.

The 08:30 departure to Norwich prepares to leave Liverpool Street during the Queen's Silver Jubilee in1977. Named 'The Jubilee', the train in this picture was to be in the charge of four trainee drivers that were undergoing brake handling trials, one of them being me. The three men on the far right of the picture were driver instructors and were, from left to right, Tom Blackburn, Dick Dunbar and Peter Fowkes. As a matter of interest, the Union Jack flag was later re-painted to show the correct version.

Table showing the various types of traction units that I eventually became qualified to drive.

Type of Unit	Training Centre	Date from	Date to	Date passed
Class 37 English Electric	Ilford School	19th January 1976	28th Jan. 1976	28th January 1976
Class 47 Brush Sulzer	Ilford School	14th February 1977	15th April 1977	26th July 1977
Class 08/0 English Electric	Stratford	8th August 1977	12th August 1977	12th August 1977
Class 08/1 (Conversion)	Stratford	11th August 1977	11th August 1977	11th August 1977
Class 31/ 1&4 Brush	Stratford	3rd September 1977	9th September 1977	9th September 1977
Class 31/0 (conversion)	Stratford	12th September 1977	16th September 1977	16th September 1977
Class 37 (conversion)	Stratford	19th September 1977	23rd September 1977	23rd September 1977
Basic Diesel Multiple Unit	Ilford School	31st October 1977	18th November 1977	16th December 1977
Basic Electric Multiple Unit	Ilford School	5th June 1978	16th June 1978	4th July 1978
312 / 306 EMU conversion	Ilford School	26th June 1978	30th June 1978	7th July 1978
315 EMU (conversion)	Ilford School	26th September 1983	30th September 1983	30th September 1983
310 EMU (conversion)	Ilford School	15th June 1987	18th June 1987	19th June 1987
321 / 322 EMU conversion	Cambridge	14th December 1988	15th December 1988	31st January 1989
317 EMU (conversion)	Cambridge	11th November 1989	--	11th November 1989
Class 97 Battery loco.	Ilford School	19th March 1990	23rd March 1990	18th June 1990
313 EMU (conversion)	Hornsey	15th February 1993	16th February 1993	27th April 1993

Class-47 locomotive named *County of Hertfordshire* sits in platform 9 at Liverpool Street waiting to work an express to Norwich. The colourful large logo livery was applied by Stratford in July 1981 in connection with the Royal wedding of HRH Prince of Wales and Lady Diana Spencer. I was the secondman on this service.

having to work night shifts. On one particular night, we were training on Class 31s, working a freight train to and from Parkeston Quay. There were three of us along with the driver instructor (only four people were ever allowed in a cab at any one time), and the weather on this night had started out fairly wet and windy. On our return trip, the weather took a turn for the worse, and as we were passing through the outskirts of Brentwood, the rain started to fall in torrents. Almost on cue, a thunderstorm began and the water cascaded from the embankment retaining walls at Brentwood like waterfalls. As we rounded the curve towards Harold Wood, we could see the

Diesel shunting loco number 08 320 is seen at Liverpool Street's platform 14, moving a rake of Mk.1 rolling stock under the Primrose Street bridge in the late 1970s.

lightning striking the ground ahead of our train in the Gidea Park area. Each flash lit up our worried faces in the darkness of the cab, all of us wondering whether we would make it back to Stratford in one piece!

Once I had passed the relevant type of traction, time wasn't wasted in putting me to work on the Temple Mills hump shunters. In the winter months, I soon learned that taking these locomotives over the hump and onto the shunting neck, to run back to the other end of the yard, needed great care approaching the buffer stops on the falling gradient. These locos were very prone to skidding in the frosty conditions. Another place that I worked on these '350s' was on the Liverpool Street shunting loco, commonly called the station pilot. The drivers of this locomotive usually took great pride in keeping it in tip-top condition, and were actually allowed an hour's overtime payment to maintain the engine in a spotless state. Some keen drivers even went to the effort of polishing the copper pipework within the cab. The station pilot's job was mainly to release locomotives from the buffer-stop end of platforms, to enable them to work other trains or travel back to Stratford depot. Otherwise, they shunted parcel vans from one service to another.

Around this time in my career, attempts were brought in to have selected trains driven under the single manning arrangement; that is, just the driver and the guard, but no second man in the cab. This had always been the case with suburban electric multiple units, but it was a new idea to have locomotive hauled trains driven in this way. With the introduction of electric train heating (ETH), the second man's job was becoming untenable. His main functions were to couple and uncouple the locomotive from the train, alter the headcode on the front of the loco, assist the driver in maintaining a good look-out for signals, and attend to the train-heating boiler during the winter months. With the removal of the headcode blinds, this job no longer existed. Shunters were stationed at main terminals, so they were quite capable of attaching and detaching the locomotives. With the

An unidentified Class 37 heads an up Cambridge service into the rural station of Elsenham, an Essex village well known for its world-famous jams. Note the wooden level crossing, and the lack of any extra means of preventing passengers crossing the tracks at will. Note also, the signalman's VW car parked in the spot that marked where an old cattle-loading platform used to be located, near the rear of the train.

A busy scene at Cambridge station, with a King's Lynn service arriving from Liverpool Street at platform 4, passing a terminating service standing in platform 1. Note that the headcode indicator boxes had all been changed to white dots. These were the services that I liked working best, be it as a secondman or a driver.

A close-up study of a Class 37 locomotive standing in the holding sidings at London's Liverpool Street station. The chain that can be seen near the steps is part of the handbrake arrangement, and was taut if the brake was screwed on at that end. Handbrakes were required because when the locomotive was shut down, the air system slowly leaked away, rendering the locomotive brake-less. If the loco happened to be parked on even the slightest gradient, it would be able to roll away! Note also, the old bullhead rail that was still quite prevalent in yards and sidings, and sometimes on some main lines!

introduction of colour-light signals on a lot of the main line routes, and the fact that most diesel locomotive cabs gave a good view ahead, the driver could see what he needed to see without assistance. This meant that the second man was, in the end, just a glorified boiler attendant, until the full introduction of ETH took place. This brought about an interesting situation. How on earth were future drivers going to gain their practical experience?

I was given a driving turn under the single manning arrangement one day when I was spare duty. Someone had gone sick, so I had to take up his job. This involved travelling up to London, then working the 04:05 Peterborough parcel train service as far as Cambridge and return with the 07:48 passenger train to Liverpool Street. The locomotive was already attached to the parcel vans at Liverpool Street, and a Cambridge driver took over on my arrival at Cambridge. It felt very strange to be in the cab of a class 47 locomotive and working the train by oneself, with the guard riding within the train. Luckily, the return trip did not involve many stops, with the train calling only at Audley End, Bishop's Stortford and Liverpool Street, where we arrived at 09:03. It was rare for hauled services to stop at Tottenham Hale in those days, with only 1L19, the 08:06 up stopping service from Cambridge, booked to stop there at 09:26 in the morning peak.

Driving a locomotive hauled train was certainly a skilful job, be it passenger or freight trains, and the only way to acquire this ability was through experience. I managed to gain my knowledge, thanks to the many drivers who had let me take to the controls of their trains as a driver's assistant. It was sometimes stated that anyone could make the train 'go', it was the stopping that needed the skill. In the end, I was able to demonstrate text book 'one brake application' station stops with passenger trains, especially on the Norwich expresses. I had this down to perfection on the Up approach to Colchester station. If everything was running to schedule, the approach to Colchester was made at a speed of between 85 and 90 miles per hour. As the train passed over the Clacton branch-line bridge, the brake valve was placed in the 'initial' brake application position, to set up the train's air brake distributors (the equivalent to the old-fashioned triple valves). As the train neared the point where the falling gradient changed to a rising one, a 'full service' application was made until a substantial 'bite' could be felt and the brake valve returned to the 'lap' position. As the train entered the platform at approximately forty miles per hour, the brake valve was then placed in the 'release' position. On the surface, it appeared that the train may be about to over-run the platform, and on many an occasion I could sense my co-driver's toes curling up in his shoes. With the aid of the rising gradient, the brakes slowly released, and the train was brought to a smooth stand at the London-end of the platform. Then, just a light application on the independent brake valve was made to hold the train steady whilst at a stand.

The art came in having the confidence in the equipment that one was using, and also in applying the rule of performing what was called a 'running brake test' on the initial start of the journey. Before a train left any terminal, a static brake test was carried out to ensure the continuity of the braking system, whether it was the old vacuum brakes or air brakes. This ensured that all the relevant pipes and hoses were connected and in working order. It was then the driver's job to ascertain the 'feel' of the brakes once the train had reached a reasonable speed, and this test was to be carried out well before reaching the first junction or stopping point. During periods of freezing weather conditions, these running brake tests were carried out at intervals of every three to five minutes to guard against the air brakes freezing up.

Due to the shortage of drivers at Stratford, I soon moved into what was known as the railcar link, which was a step up from the shunting link. This involved working the Diesel Multiple Units to places such as Southminster off the Southend branch, Stratford to North Woolwich, and Upminster from Romford. These 'Romford - Upminster' jobs must have been some of the most monotonous jobs going, with about twelve round trips being performed in a shift. There was only one station between the two terminating points, at Emerson Park. Occasionally, we also worked the last train as far as Bishop's Stortford on the Cambridge line with these units, especially when the overhead power lines were switched off to be worked upon. In one respect, I was glad to see the back of the '350' shunting locos, as their riding qualities were very rough. In my opinion, they were just one step away from being like a steam locomotive, complete with side rods, but without the fire and steam. The move from a shunting link straight into a passenger link always seemed strange to me. Here was a novice driver, probably not long having passed his driving exams, being able to take charge of passenger-carrying trains. The rigorous exams should have made sure that the person concerned was quite capable of driving any particular train that they were qualified to drive.

I started to learn the DMUs on 31st October 1977, and in the end was conversant with Classes 104, 105, and 116. Shortly after this in November, my daughter Anne was born - a second addition to the family. While I was based at Stratford, there was a class of railcar that had Rolls Royce engines fitted and fluid torque-converter drives, like the ones I was used to in Australia, but the ones that I learned to drive had British Universal Traction engines. These were a Leyland engine rated at 150 horsepower, with a mechanical gearbox. This meant that the driver actually had to change gear at certain intervals to get up to top speed. The brakes on these units were vacuum operated. Because of the railcar knowledge that I had gained, it meant that locomotive work was going to become less frequent, unless I was booked spare duty and received the work that way.

I liked working with the Class 116 units, as they were slightly larger and heavier than their 105 counterparts. The 116s were also better to work with during rush hours, due to the fact that more doors were fitted to these units, enabling commuters to board and alight with more ease.

People had often said that the first driving turn on the main line on your own would be the most nerve wracking, especially in the dark, where any red light spotted along the line could be mistaken for a red signal. My nerves were tested on my first day by an air gauge showing 'zero', rather than a trackside red light. My first driving turn with the 116 railcars involved working an empty set from Stratford to Wickford to start the day's service on the Southminster line. As I was trundling along in the dark, somewhere the other side of Gidea Park, my heart gave a start when I noticed a gauge in front of me showing zero! My mind was soon put to rest when I realised it was the brake cylinder gauge, which would naturally show zero when the train was on the move. After spending about five months working various shifts on the railcars, the call came for me to learn the Electric Multiple Units. I resisted this for as long as I possibly could, because I couldn't stand working with electric trains. To me they were lifeless machines that had no character whatsoever.

On the 5th June 1978, I returned to the Ilford Training school to begin my training on the dreaded Electric Multiple Units. This started off with basic lectures about electricity and how traction units used it, and also general rules relating to safely working with 25,000 volts. I then went on to learn the basic multiple units, which started with the following Classes; four-car 302s, which were utilised on the Fenchurch Street

> On the surface, it appeared that the train may be about to over-run the platform, and on many an occasions I could sense my co-driver's toes curling up in his shoes.

Just to show that not all Cambridge services were dominated by Class 37s, a Class 31 with an Up Cambridge service is seen arriving at platform 2 at Bishop's Stortford in the early 1980s. The yellow disc signal seen in the foreground allowed drivers to pass it like this for shunting movements, but it needed to be rotated 45° before it gave them permission to move onto the main line. Note the small semaphore signal that let trains into the yard, on the left of the picture.

An Up Cambridge service, in the charge of a Class 31 locomotive, calls at Elsenham station on its way towards Liverpool Street. This station has won numerous awards for Best Kept Station due to the tireless efforts of its staff maintaining the gardens. Moving into the railcar link meant that this kind of work would become less frequent for me. Stratford driver Joe Bygrave was in the secondman's seat while he allows his assistant to drive the train under instruction. Joe eventually transferred to Bishop's Stortford depot.

A very wintry scene at North Woolwich, with a two-car 105 set waiting to return to Stratford. Note that by this stage, the additional goods line had been taken up about 400 yards short of the station. Freight trains only went as far as Silvertown and shunted the factories in that vicinity.

The cab view of the Class 116 DMU showing the main controls that were within reach of the driver. They were as follows:- 1, track-circuit-operating clips; 2, engine running lights; 3, window wiper control; 4, throttle handle; 5, AWS cancelling button; 6, two-tone horn lever; 7, gear selector; 8, reverser handle; 9, AWS indicator; 10, drivers brake valve (just out of sight).

to Shoeburyness line, three-car 305s, which were used on the suburban lines to Chingford, Enfield and Hertford East, four-car 305/2s, which were employed on the Bishop's Stortford services, three-car 306s that were for the Shenfield suburban services, and the four-car 307s which were mainly used on the Southend Victoria outer suburban services. There was a lot to take in regarding the various differences between these units, and when it came round to taking my traction exam on these trains, I did my best to appear that I didn't know a lot about them. I just didn't fancy being stuck driving these trains forever more, as I preferred the diesel locomotive work. Needless to say, the examiners saw through my charade and passed me as competent to drive these machines. It now meant that most of the time I was driving electric trains or the railcars, and the locomotive work was becoming a thing of the past. Most of the work entailed driving on the Stratford to Woolwich shuttle services and eventually, in the summer of 1979, we gained some jobs that extended these workings to Camden Road, which broke the monotony somewhat. These services became known as the Crosstown Link Line.

A green-liveried Class 104 DMU sits on the shed at Stratford in 1972. These units were built by the Birmingham Railway Carriage & Wagon Company in 1957 to 1959 and featured the British Universal Traction engine, rated at 150 horsepower.

A 104 Class two-car diesel multiple unit is seen arriving at the north end of Cambridge station with a service or Peterborough. Note the Class 37 locomotive standing in the holding sidings at the end of the platform.

A Derby-built Class 116 three-car Diesel Multiple Unit stands at Southend Victoria whilst being used by the author and his fellow drivers for brake training trips between here and Wickford. This view shows why these vehicles were best suited for commuter work, with the amount of extra doors on each car.

A three-car Class 116 DMU sits at Southminster, waiting for me to drive the return shuttle service to Wickford. Freight trains also used Southminster; one service was the sand train service to Mile End in London, the other was the British Nuclear Fuels train that hauled the nuclear flask carrying waste from the reactor at Sizewell, which was situated on the east coast.

A two-car 105 DMU passes the site that was being earmarked for the M11 motorway extension, near Elsenham, on its way to Bishop's Stortford with the local stopping service from Cambridge.

In the summer of 1978, I was trained on the 312 Class electrics and, along with their 310 counterparts, were the most popular types of multiple units that I have had the chance to drive. Their cabs were roomy, and the suspension on these units was firm but smooth to ride on. The 312s were capable of running at 90 mph, whereas the 310s were 75 mph units. The 310 units were introduced in 1965 for use on the Euston suburban services on the Midland main line and were built at Derby. The 312 units were built following the electrification of the King's Cross outer suburban area and were built at York. The units that were specifically built for the ex-Great Eastern were numbered 312 718 to 312 799 and were all allocated to Clacton depot.

In the lead-up to the Christmas of 1978, my domestic life started to show signs of cracking around the edges. It was hinted at that my children didn't know that they had a father, because I spent so much time away from home. If I wasn't at work, then I was in bed trying to catch up on much needed rest. Very often, it was literally a case of work, sleep, work, sleep. On the rare day off, I was often out with the lads on the trusty old BSA, just to unwind. If I was to save my relationship, I had to think of a way around the problem of having to travel about 35 miles to work every day. The answer lay in a transfer to a depot nearer to my home, and this only meant one place; Bishop's Stortford. This would alleviate the need to spend a lot of time travelling to and from work, as the depot was a ten-minute train journey away. In times when there was no train service, I could always use my motorcycle. If I was feeling really fit, I could always fall back on my trusty push-bike. I didn't really want to leave the locomotive work behind, and transferring to Bishop's Stortford meant that the work would be solely driving electric trains. With my marriage suffering, I was left with no other choice, so I duly lodged my application to be transferred to Bishop's Stortford and sat back and waited for the acknowledgement.

Sitting back was not quite the right words, as by this stage I had learned the Class 309 electrics which were utilised on the Walton and Clacton outer suburban services. This meant that at some stage I would need to learn the road to these two places on the Essex coast. A transfer could sometimes take many months

A preserved example of the 306 Class Electric Multiple Units that I learned to drive in the summer of 1978. When I first encountered these units they were painted in the all-over corporate blue livery of British Rail. This unit is seen at Ilford Car Sheds, repainted in the LNER green.

to take place, depending on vacancies occurring at the place requested. I must admit that I had not done any research in placing my transfer request for Bishop's Stortford, preferring to take pot luck. Had I done so, I would have discovered when the next person was due to retire at that depot. Almost on cue, about a month before my transfer actually came through, (a lot faster than I had anticipated), I was given a couple of weeks to learn the route from Colchester to Walton-on-the-Naze and Clacton,

On the left is the badge I designed for ASLEF District No. 1's 100 years of existence. The two locomotives featured also showed how far rail travel had progressed. In the centre is the same design as used by District Council No. 5 in 1984. On the right is the Southern Region's copy for the centenary of ASLEF.

including St. Botolphs, which is now known as Colchester Town. Someone in the admin office was either being very kind, or had obviously not done their homework. By the time had elapsed after completing the route learning, my transfer to 'Stortford was about to take place.

About two months before I left Stratford depot, I was approached by Lew Adams, the local representative of the train driver's union, ASLEF, (later to become the ASLEF General Secretary) and asked if I could design a badge that would be used for the District Number One's centenary celebrations the following year. The Associated Society of Locomotive Engineers and Firemen was formed in 1880 to exclusively protect and enhance the rights of footplate men in the workplace. I had joined this union when I first started on the railways in 1970, and Lew had known about my artistic abilities for some time. I wracked my brain for a suitable design.

British Rail had been running 100mph services from King's Cross using the 3,000hp 'Deltic' locomotives, but in 1974, they introduced even higher speeds on the King's Cross to Scotland main line in the form of the InterCity 125s. These units had a power car at each end of a set seven or nine-car formation. I decided to incorporate an image of one of these units and stand it next to a design representing Stephenson's Rocket. Whilst strictly more than a hundred years had passed between the building of the two, it represented the progress man had made in rail travel. The design was also used by District Council number five in 1984 to commemorate their centenary. The design was so well liked that the Southern Region ASLEF copied the design, replacing the red circular outer band with a pale green colour.

I left Stratford in December 1979, and the depot still boasted a fleet of 138 locomotives. They consisted of 39 Class 47s, 24 Class 37s, 30 Class 31s, 39 Class 08 shunting locos and six Class 03 Drewry shunting locos. As for the train crews, there were 460 drivers and 227 secondmen still employed, whereas there were 663 maintenance staff. My transfer to Bishop's Stortford took place on the 12th December, 1979. I was given a brief introductory interview at the Area Manager's office located at Broxbourne, and was asked the question as to what route knowledge I would require. Without thinking, I replied that I didn't need any as I already signed the relevant routes for the depot. In hindsight, I could have gained a few days grace to gradually break me in to the new depot's routines. As it happened, I was out driving trains the very next day, with the interview day used as my 'locker day' to enable me to move all of my relevant equipment from Stratford to 'Stortford. Strangely enough, I had to hand in my hand Bardic lamp at Stratford, just to be issued with an identical lamp at Bishop's Stortford. (That's the Railway bureaucracy for you). These lamps were part of train crews' essential equipment that was to be carried with us whilst on duty. They were capable of showing red, green and yellow lights as well as the normal white light. The green light was used by the guard on hauled services to give a driver the 'right-away' from stations, whereas the yellow was used by permanent-way staff to slow trains for an emergency speed restriction (no longer used) or to authorise a driver to pass a colour-light signal at danger. A bracket on the rear allowed the lamp to be used as a tail lamp in emergencies. The only drawback

An eight-car 312 Class Electric Multiple Unit rolls into Shenfield on the down main line on its way to Clacton. The train is seen in its original all-over blue British Rail corporate livery.

The east side of Liverpool Street station in the 1970s sees a 312 Class unit in the new blue and grey livery standing in platform 13, waiting to work a Clacton service, while a 307 unit can be seen just beyond on a Southend service. The buildings in the background were eventually demolished when the station was redeveloped in 1990. One of these buildings was the public house known as the 'Black Raven', a popular haunt of bikers and Teddy Boys in the late 1960s and early 70s.

with the lamps was their size and weight. With all of the other equipment that drivers had to carry whilst on duty, this made their bags extremely heavy (I weighed mine and it was 20lb!), and this sometimes lead to neck and shoulder strain.

Once I arrived at Bishop's Stortford depot, I noticed that there was a shunting job involving the use of a '350' shunting locomotive. This was the Harlow Mill yard pilot, which was used for shunting sand wagons up an incline to the United Glass factory, as well as general shunting of vans from goods trains,

dropping off vehicles for the warehouse located in the yard. This job was in the normal roster, but eventually became a job for drivers that were medically restricted from running on the main line. One of these particular drivers, the late Roy Swain, kept the locomotive spick and span, even down to polishing the internal copper pipework and lining the external battery boxes. The locomotive was given white buffers and a white roof, similar to the Stratford 47s. He gave the regular loco, 08 520, the name of Duchess of Harlow and I helped to tidy up the

An example of a Bardic Lamp, as used by drivers and guards for train working purposes. The bracket on the rear allowed it to be used as a tail lamp in emergencies. These lamps are slowly being phased out for smaller and lighter versions similar to bicycle lamps.

Seen above is the 08 Class shunting loco that was stationed at Harlow Mill, complete with the white cab roof and buffers. Numbered 08 520, it was named *Duchess Of Harlow* by its regular driver, Roy Swain. The close-up shows the lettering that was tidied up by me.

The view of Walton-on-the-Naze signal box, looking towards London. This picture was taken when the author was learning the route to here and Clacton-on-Sea, and taking photographs aided this learning process. In the siding on the left is a Class 308 Electric Multiple Unit. The main semaphore arm took trains towards Frinton-on-Sea and London, and the disc signal was for trains entering the Down Sidings, seen in the distance.

A 309 Class 'Clacton' unit stands at Walton-on-the-Naze awaiting it return journey to Liverpool Street. Note that the front windows were of the curved type, later modified for squarer types that were cheaper to replace.

A view from the Up Goods Loop at Harlow Mill looking west. In the centre of the picture is the incline that led to the United Glass works. The area on the left, behind the gasometers, is now occupied by a car showroom and servicing workshops.

A close-up view of the incline that led to the United Glass works, once known as Key Glass. Just to the right of the gate, a ground-level searchlight signal can be seen. This signal would allow freight trains onto the main line from the goods loop.

lettering with my sign-writing skills.

Roy Swain was one of those many railway characters that grew up with steam traction and, upon dieselisation, found it hard to shake off the habits of a steam locomotive driver. This became evident when they were required to wear a driver's uniform, preferring instead to wear the denim overalls and peaked cap that was the favourite of steam men. Stratford depot also had its fair share of 'characters' and, apart from Tony Gooding already mentioned, another notable individual from Stratford was Brian Andrews, a typical east-end cockney. He would appear for duty in his overalls, with flat cap, cravat and hob-nailed boots, complete with a long beard and the remains of a roll-up cigarette on his lips.

Bishop's Stortford station was geographically located on an 'S' curve on the London to Cambridge main line, and the track speed through the station was limited to 45 miles per hour. The carriage sidings were located on the Up London-side of the station and were capable of storing eight Electric Multiple Units, which equated to 32 carriages. It was here that the units were cleaned and water tanks refilled, ready for the next days' duties. Behind the signal box on the Down side were the freight sidings, mostly handling local coal traffic as well as the banana vans for the Geest factory at Easton Lodge.

The coal traffic eventually ceased to be shipped by rail, and the yard was converted to make use of aggregate stone traffic.

On the left is the badge issued to drivers that were members of ASLEF, the train drivers union, to mark their 10 years of loyalty.

On the right is the badge that I designed to commemorate the 1982 strike that Bishop's Stortford Depot took part in.

The badge that I designed for the Bishop's Stortford half-century membership of ASLEF is seen on the left, featuring an L1 locomotive and 30C shed plate.

This traffic in turn was moved to the Harlow Mill yard, under the Yeoman Aggregates banner. Eventually, Harlow Mill saw three different stone trains use the facilities there on Tuesdays and Thursdays.

The 1980s seemed to pass by quite quickly, though it heralded an era of great change within the industry, as well as at home. In 1980, I received my 10-year loyalty badge from ASLEF, marking my 10 years on the railways.

The early part of 1981 was taken up by the discussion of introducing single-manning on trains, which turned into a full-scale strike in 1982. This started out with the introduction of Flexible Rostering, which basically involved moving away from the traditional eight-hour day and 40 hour week. Shifts were to be altered so they lasted anywhere between seven to nine hours. Also, new recruits to the footplate were to be taken from a 'trainman concept', which were to bring guards and drivers into one common line of promotion. The secondman's job in the cab was no longer necessary, except on trains that were to travel over 100 miles per hour. This created an uproar with the drivers union ASLEF, but as I have already mentioned, the secondman was becoming just a glorified boiler attendant, and I was already used to working very flexible shift lengths in Australia. Besides, with the abolition of the secondman's job, new drivers had to be obtained from somewhere, and the railways preferred to recruit from within the industry rather than take on new people 'off the street'. British Rail also wanted to introduce open stations where there were no staff on duty at all, and no way of collecting revenue from the travelling public. The unions considered this to be an unsafe move, putting the travelling public at risk during the hours of darkness from loitering youths.

By the summer of 1982 there was a two-pronged attack upon the driver's union, with the Government joining forces with British Rail Chairman, Sir Peter Parker, to try and destroy the 'recalcitrant' ASLEF. The plan was to threaten drivers that had been on strike by issuing them with a notice of dismissal, and that they would only be offered their jobs back if they were no longer members of ASLEF. The plan would have brought the railway management and the government into conflict with the whole trade union movement. Bishop's Stortford depot was on strike for just over a fortnight in 1982 before the strike was concluded. In the meantime, with no wages coming in, I had to make my own way over to the local Social Security office in Braintree, to claim benefits to maintain my family, which had by now had an additional daughter born in 1981. I was eventually asked to design a badge to commemorate the 'battle', as did all other depots around the country. My design (seen left) incorporated an outline of a Class 305/2 slam-door unit with a silhouette of the Bishop's Stortford church in the background.

A plate was made by ASLEF for the Great Eastern section,

Ex Bishop's Stortford driver Roy Swain, who became responsible for the decoration of the Harlow Mill shunting locomotive 08 520 with the name *Duchess of Harlow*. He is seen here in the cab of his beloved Foden 'D' type steam tractor timber road vehicle, of which there were only 10 operational vehicles left in the country at the time of writing. His career with the railways started at Enfield Town, where he became one of the country's youngest firemen that was passed for driving duties at the age of nineteen. From Enfield Town, he transferred to King's Cross, then Stratford, and eventually Bishop's Stortford, where he saw the end of steam traction. Roy left the footplate on ill-health grounds, spending the last days of his career as a crossing keeper at Elsenham's level crossing, living in the station house nearby. He sadly passed away on 20th July 1996, doing the thing he enjoyed the most; attending a steam rally at Weeting in Suffolk. MICHAEL SWAIN

Two of the different types of Electric Multiple Units that I would be driving on a regular basis once I had transferred to Bishop's Stortford depot. The 302 Class, is seen above in platform 3 at Bishop's Stortford, normally found on the Southend line, whilst below is the 305/2 Class at the same location, with the author's brother leaning out of the first window.

Scenes around Bishop's Stortford in the 1970s

Not a 'Toffee Apple' Brush but a 'blue star' Class 31 (number 31 109) with destination discs on the front, seen here arriving at Bishop's Stortford with a Cambridge service. The train is just passing over the connections with the Down Yard from the Up main line.

A 1970s scene at Bishop's Stortford, looking towards the station from what was the A11 road bridge. Although in a track-circuit area, semaphore signals can be seen in the goods yard on the left. The disc signal in the foreground has a small diamond symbol on it, signifying that the signalman would know of a train's presence at the signal.

Pictured above is a loading gauge in the Down goods yard at Bishop's Stortford, with St. Michael's church in the background. These gauges were used to ensure that the loading in an open vehicle did not exceed a certain limit due to the clearance under low bridges. This gauge could be swung away from the track that it applied to.

The rear view of Bishop's Stortford signal box, a view not often seen by the everyday commuter, complete with the signalman's car and a tidy heap of coal for the box's coal-burning stove. The box was named Bishop's Stortford South, as there used to be another box at the country-end of platform one in the steam days.

Above is the plate that was made to commemorate all of the Great Eastern depots that took part in the strike action in the summer of 1982. The badges shown, clockwise from the top are as follows:- Chingford, Bishop's Stortford, Enfield Town, Norwich, N.E.London, Ipswich, Stratford, Cambridge, King's Lynn, Parkeston, Great Eastern, London Tilbury & Southend, March, Hertford East, Lowestoft, and Broad Street. The plate is now a collector's item.

The look of concentration is evident in this interior view of a Class 305/2 slam-door EMU cab. My right hand is resting on the Driver's Safety Device, otherwise known as the Deadman's handle. Just above this can be seen the basic means of communication with the guard, with one button being a buzzer and the other being pressed when talking into the mouthpiece.

which depicted badges produced by all of the depots that were currently open at the time that took part in the strike, and is pictured on page 98. The plate is now a collector's item.

Shortly after the 1982 strike had been cleared up, I was asked if I would like to take up a position as the Assistant Secretary for the Bishop's Stortford Branch of ASLEF, working alongside Secretary Don Sutton. I was duly elected for the post in 1984 and soon after, I was asked to design a badge that was going be used commemorate Bishop's Stortford's 50-year membership of ASLEF. I decided to use a profile of an L1 steam locomotive that was prevalent at the depot in the steam days, along with the number representing the shed plates carried by locomotives, which was 30C for Bishop's Stortford. The final design chosen is seen on page 93. (The railway had actually reached as far as Bishop's Stortford in 1842). Prior to its 1936 independence as a branch of ASLEF, 'Stortford had looked to Cambridge for union matters.

Towards the end of 1984, preparatory work was started on the raising or modifying of road bridges that crossed railway lines between Bishop's Stortford and Cambridge. This was in readiness for the possible electrification of this section of line, but it wasn't until the summer of 1985 that discussions took place between rail chiefs and Cambridge County Council with a view to electrifying the railway line between Bishop's Stortford and Cambridge, including the section of line between Royston and Cambridge on the Great Northern line. Some of the bridges involved had part of the masonry arches demolished to make way for new pre-cast concrete structures. Their overall height was raised by just over 300mm to accommodate the 25kv electric overhead wires above the track.

Whilst the bridge work was being undertaken, the signalling between Bishop's Stortford was upgraded to full four-aspect status. Previously, although the signals had been of the colour-light searchlight type, they were more or less configured to the semaphore arrangements, where there were distant, home and starting signals for each station. Each station had been equipped with a signal box, and the system had non-standard signals in some places. The Down Distant for the Intermediate Block signal between Elsenham and Newport for instance, although it looked like a colour-light signal the yellow and green shade behind the lens was on a semaphore arm! Also, the signal that guarded the entrance to Audley End tunnel on the Down Line had been approach-lit, which meant that most of the time it was out (not lit) until an approaching train occupied a particular electrical track circuit.

Between the years 1983 and 1988, I was trained on how to drive the 315, 310 and 321 Electric Multiple Units. The 310s and 321s were eventually utilised on the newly electrified Cambridge services. The only drawback with these units, from a ticket inspector's point of view, was the fully enclosed cab. This meant that a through connection was not available between two units. The guard that worked each train usually worked from the rear unit, with internal verbal and bell or buzzer communication available with the driver. The 315s came virtually ready-equipped for Driver Only Operation, with the door control button spaces already allowed for on the driver's desk. The guard had a panel by each crew door for the normal opening and closing of doors.

In the mid-1980s, I endured a couple of traumatic events that changed the course of my home life, but luckily didn't interfere with my work. One day I had rode into work on my old BSA motorbike for an early start, and had volunteered for some overtime covering the afternoon shunting job. This involved bringing a train out of the Up sidings and into platform three ready for a service to London. In between my morning shift and the shunting, I had an urgent dental appointment for the extraction of two teeth. Over the previous week-end, I had cracked a couple of ribs during some over-exuberant horseplay with my mates, so I wasn't looking forward to the dentist appointment. I decided to ride up to the dentists' on my BSA, and on returning back to the station, I decided to park it on platform 1 near the stairs to our mess room. Normally I would have chained it to one of the canopy posts, and colleagues used to joke that the size of the chain would have suited the Queen Mary! On this particular occasion I decided not to chain the bike, as I only had a couple of hours to go before the end of my shift.

As I sat upstairs relaxing and trying to drink a cup of tea with a numb mouth, I heard a large motorcycle being started up just below our mess room window. I walked over to have a

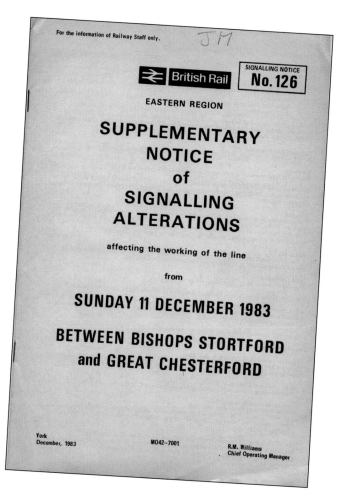

Reproduced above is the signaling notice number 126 that was issued to drivers informing them of the changes to the signals between Bishop's Stortford and Great Chesterford, dated 11th December 1983.

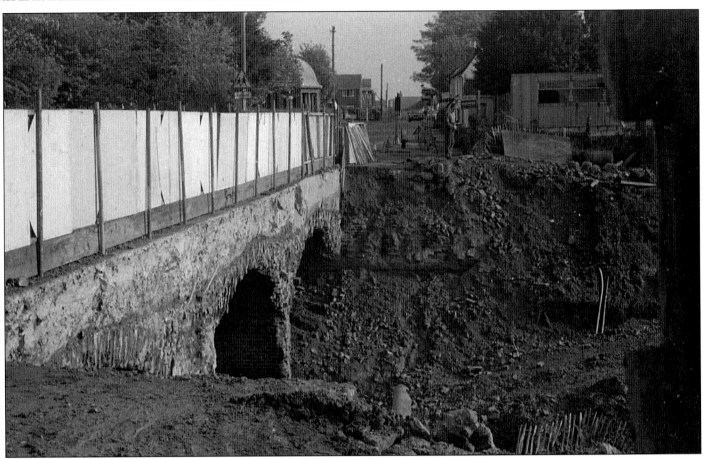

Work being undertaken on the B1051 (Stansted to Thaxted) road bridge in Elsenham, to widen and raise the structure in readiness for the electrification of the railway between Bishop's Stortford and Cambridge. The bridge dates from 1845, when the line was first opened between these two points. The camera is facing east in this picture taken in October 1984.

In the days before the overhead wires had reached this far, a Class 8 freight train passes Elsenham signal box with a train from Whitemoor to Temple Mills in the early 1970s. Note the enamel station sign, which was still in the Eastern Region blue, and the totem sign on the signal box front wall. Passengers can no longer change here for the branch line to Thaxted, as it closed in 1952.

look, just in time to see my BSA being rode off by some bloke with curly black hair. My jaw dropped to the floor and it took a few seconds for the fact to sink in that my bike had just been stolen from right under my nose! I staggered down the stairs and out to the station forecourt, thinking that perhaps one of my mates was larking around and that any minute, the bike would be rode back. Not so. I hobbled through the town, complete with a painful chest and numb mouth, trying to trace the path that the bike thief would have taken, and headed for the Police Station. As I stood at the front desk reporting the matter, the local engineer that used to service my bike pulled up outside the doors and pointed out that the bike had just been spotted going along a local road.

To cut a long story short, the bike was never recovered,

My replacement motorcycle, a Triumph T140E Bonneville, with a Hurricane tank and seat unit, which required a loan to be able to buy.

My faithful old 1951 BSA A10 Golden Flash that was eventually stolen from Bishop's Stortford railway station.

and the culprit never apprehended. The problem with the old BSA was the fact that no ignition key was needed to be able to start the bike. What galled me was the fact that the man was drunk, had no crash helmet, and had obviously sped through a busy town centre totally unnoticed! To add insult to injury, he apparently panicked on arrival at his home and proceeded to dismantle the bike, eventually throwing the parts into the River Stort.

In the meantime, while the insurance company was making its mind up about making a payout, I was forced to either sleep at work overnight for very early shifts, or walk the six miles in to work because I had no pushbike. The railways in those days were not very flexible about providing taxis to get employees in

A picture of me bringing an eight-car train from Cambridge into Elsenham station, with a 310 unit numbered 087. Despite my loathing of electric traction, these units became my favourite type due to the smooth ride available and the roomy cabs.

An unidentified Class 37 locomotive hauls a Liverpool Street to Cambridge service up the foot of Elsenham bank, complete with a buffet service, past the M11 construction site in approximately 1981. The new junction for the Stansted Airport Link, from the Cambridge direction, would eventually be built approximately where the buffet car can be seen (fourth carriage from the loco). Durrels Wood is the left of the picture.

The two-car Class 97 battery locomotive is seen at Stratford station during one of the training trips for drivers that were to assist with the electrification of the Stansted Airport tunnel. This machine was normally stabled at Hornsey depot on the Great Northern, and the training trips around the Stratford area were required to enable the drivers to gain experience with the controls and braking characteristics.

One of the new 322 units, in the Network SouthEast Stansted Express livery, coasts along the Stansted Airport branch towards the M11 road bridge. The train has just passed over the 1 in 88 falling gradient, and is now on a 1 in 253 falling gradient.

The sign erected by a local land owner, making his views known about the new expansion of Stansted Airport in 1990.

A view of the enthusiast's special, the 'Nuclear Flyer' as it starts the climb on the 1 in 88 gradient towards the Stansted Airport tunnel.

to work. The walk from Elsenham to Bishop's Stortford used to take me about an hour and twenty-five minutes, but I was able to improve this to one hour and five minutes in the end!

Alas, pressures with my home life were building up, and my wife calmly informed me one day that she had filed for divorce, citing unreasonable behaviour as the cause. At first I treated this statement with disbelief, until the official papers dropped onto my doormat. Whilst I admit there were faults on both sides, there seemed to be no way of patching things up, especially once the divorce solicitors had got their claws on the case. By the August of 1985, I could see that I was wasting my time, and left the marital home to live in a rented room five minutes away from my depot. With no turning back, my divorce became absolute in January of 1986.

Later that year, I was in a position to rent a flat in Bishop's Stortford, sharing the costs with a work colleague. In the early part of 1987, I tentatively started a new relationship which resulted in my second marriage in 1988.

Around about the same time upon the railways, work was under way to construct a railway line from Stansted Mountfitchet to Stansted Airport, one of London's up-and-coming provincial airports. The main junction was to be located about 500 yards north of Stansted station, swinging eastward under the now established M11 motorway, then diving into a mile-long tunnel under the runway before terminating under the main terminal building at the airport. While the tunnel was being constructed, a handful of Bishop's Stortford drivers were trained on the class 97 battery locomotives to assist with the overhead wiring trains within the tunnel. This was for health and safety reasons, to avoid excessive fumes that would be created by a diesel locomotive.

A dedicated fleet of electric units were to be utilised on the new Stansted Airport services, to be known as the Stansted Skytrain, and these were classified as 322s. They were almost identical with their 321 predecessors, but were given a special Stansted Skytrain livery, later renamed Stansted Express. The building of the Airport branch was quite an engineering feat, and necessitated a steep climb towards the tunnel due to a stream being located about a four hundred yards before the tunnel entrance. The line left the main line from London on a gradient of 1 in 219 then rose to 1 in 71 almost immediately, running towards the M11 motorway. The gradient eased to 1 in 253 before another climb of 1 in 88 before passing over the stream, then easing to 1 in 750 through the tunnel.

A lot of the land in the surrounding area was obtained under a compulsory-purchase order, and did not curry favour with local people, least of all the local farmer. He duly erected a large sign adjacent to the railway line, voicing the opinion that the Airport was a white elephant. I sympathised to a degree, as part of Durrels Wood (home of a local badger sett) was destroyed to make way for the railway. I found it strange that nowhere near as much fuss was made when the motorway was extended from

The original branding that was used for the new airport services.

Bishop's Stortford to Cambridge, cutting through the very same wood. As it happened, the airport expansion would secure my depot's existence for some time, as we were required to work many of the new trains to and from London.

In September 1988, Bishop's Stortford station suffered a major blaze when the overhead footbridge connecting platforms 1 and 2 caught fire whilst building contractors were working on the roof. The blaze started at about 16:30 just before the evening rush hour, and caused chaos when the 25,000-volt overhead power had to be turned off before fire-fighters could tackle the blaze, with parts of the bridge exploding and falling onto the tracks. The bridge dated back to 1960, and was being refurbished at the time.

On the 30th March 1991, not long after the new airport branch had opened, a special hauled train was allowed to traverse the line on an enthusiasts' special that had started from Worcester Shrub Hill, and went to Leiston on the east coast. Nicknamed the 'Nuclear Flyer' railtour, it called in at Stansted Airport at about 17.30 that afternoon on its return leg from Leiston. As there were no turning facilities at the airport, the train was top-and-tailed with a class 47 loco at one end and two class 37s at the other. Two pictures of this train are shown below.

Around about the same time as the Stansted Airport branch line was being built, the City of London terminal of Liverpool Street was undergoing a major face-lift. The ex-Midland terminal of Broad Street, next door to Liverpool Street, was demolished to make way for new offices that became generally known as Broadgate. The DC third-rail trains that used to run into this high-level terminus were absorbed into the North London Line services, running between Richmond and North Woolwich. It was a major engineering feat to redevelop Liverpool Street and continue to run train services in and out of the terminal while all the work was taking place. Not only was the track configuration altered, but the platforms were lengthened to accommodate twelve-car trains. The area between Worship Street bridge and the station canopy was built over, placing the station approach into total darkness.

In the October of 1990, cab radios were introduced onto the railways of West Anglia to enable drivers to have direct contact with signalmen. The signalmen were able to communicate directly with the passengers *via* the on-train public address system during emergencies, but a lot of the time they shied away from doing this, stating that they were too busy!

As was usual, the West Anglian section of the railways was often the last to receive any new rolling stock, and this applied when the 317 Electric Multiple Units were introduced. In fact, on reflection, we never received any rolling stock from 'new', (they were usually somebody else's cast-offs) except for the Class 322s for the new airport services. The 317s had originally been built in 1981 for use on the newly electrified St. Pancras to Bedford line and, being constructed from the beginning with driver only operation in mind, were instantly 'blacked' by the train driver's union ASLEF. It was not until an agreement was reached that the passenger services commenced in 1983, and in 1985, a sub-Class 317/2 were built for the Great Northern line, replacing the slam-door stock that was in use from King's Cross for services to Peterborough and Cambridge.

With all of this new technology and modernisation taking place, it would seem that things were on the up and up but, as time would tell, this would sadly not be the case.

The 'Nuclear Flyer is pictured above as it exits from the Tye Green portal, on its way back to Worcester on the 30th March 1991, after visiting the airport from Leiston on the east coast.

Photographs showing the major rebuilding of Liverpool Street Station towards the end of the 1980s. The picture above, taken from the corner of Liverpool Street and Old Broad Street, shows the new south-western corner piazza, with the old Sun Street Passage on the bottom left of the photo.

The picture above shows the construction of one of the track beds, while below that, can be seen part of the London Underground concourse.

The shape of things to come. The scene that greeted drivers of trains entering Liverpool Street on the Up Suburban lines as they exit Bishopsgate Tunnel and looked upwards; the new building just south of Worship Street that will be known simply as the Broadgate Tower, taken in June 2007. In the summer of 2008 this view was also blotted out by the area between Worship Street and Bishopsgate tunnel being built over as well.

A portrait of the No. 2 signal box at Broad Street station, (above) Liverpool Street's high level next-door neighbour, before Its closure in June 1986. This site was used for the Broadgate development. A 501Class DC (third rail) EMU sits in platform 8 on the left.

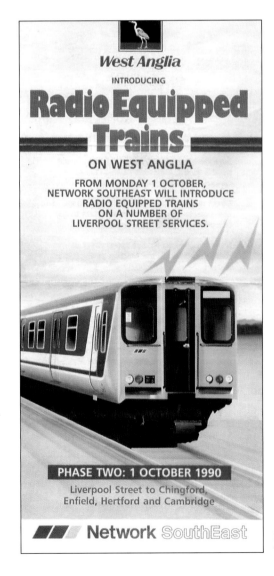

Left is the publicity leaflet advertising the new 'Radio Equipped Trains'.

CHAPTER VII
Driver Only Operation

The death knell of the railway as I knew it was sounded in 1988, with the drafting of a Traincrew Agreement regarding the running of trains with only the driver in charge. This was to be known as Driver Only Operation, abbreviated to D.O.O. for short. The way ahead for D.O.O. had been paved with the implementation of flexible rostering in the 1980s, brought in by the newly formed British Railways Board. Under the 'Sector Management' banner, it sought to break the railways into five self-regulating business sectors, which became known as Freight (eventually becoming Railfreight), Parcels (Rail Express Systems), InterCity, Provincial (Regional Railways) and London and South East (Network SouthEast). The successive Conservative Governments of the era encouraged the BR Board to strike out on extensive privatisation programs. The forerunner in the privatisation field was to be Foster Yeoman, a quarry company, when they purchased a small number of locomotives from the American General Motors' Electromotive Division. These locos became known as the Class 59s, and were wholly owned and maintained by Foster Yeoman, although they were driven by British Rail crews.

The whole idea of railway privatisation under the Government's Railway Bill was to reduce the subsidy paid towards the upkeep of running Britain's railways. Introducing D.O.O was part of this cost-cutting exercise. It had little to do with providing the regular commuter or freight customer with a better deal. In my little corner of Network SouthEast, we originally ran under a shadow franchise being known as West Anglia Great Northern, and were eventually taken over by Prism Rail in March 1997. Prism also ran Wales and West, Valley Lines and LTS Rail. WAGN railway came up with some significant changes to the branding of certain services to help identify the business with the locations that the railway served. It produced a new triangular logo to represent the geographical areas, and the new brands for the West Anglia area were as follows:- City Hopper, serving Chingford, Enfield Town, and Hertford East; Heron Line, for services to Cambridge; Fen Line, for services between Cambridge and King's Lynn; and Stansted Skytrain, dedicated to running trains between Liverpool Street and Stansted Airport.

For the introduction of D.O.O. to go ahead safely, new measures had to be brought in for the reliable despatch of trains. Doors on EMUs were air-operated sliding ones, and initially were under the control of the guard. Eventually, instead of the guard stepping onto the station platform from his train to check that passengers had boarded or alighted and that all doors were shut before the train was allowed to proceed, this became the driver's responsibility. With the guard's job being phased out on most services, mothers were expected to cope with the loading of their own children's prams. To enable the driver to monitor activity on platforms more efficiently, mirrors, cameras and monitors were to be provided at strategic locations, especially on platforms with an adverse curve. At some terminals, new technology enabled 'CD' (Close Doors) and 'RA' (Right Away) indicators to be installed. At other locations, the driver was required to lower his side droplight (window) and physically look back along the platform to monitor that passengers were joining or leaving his train safely. Over a number of years, this 'look back' method of working resulted in my suffering from shoulder, neck and back problems due to the twisting of the neck to observe passengers on the platforms, and I underwent a series of physiotherapy sessions to ease the problem.

To the average man in the street, it appeared that drivers were giving up very little for a new pay rise associated with the new D.O.O. working practices, but the fact of the matter remained that the guard's vital safety role of being there to protect the rear of the train in the event of a mishap was being taken away. This meant that in any mishap, it was solely the driver's responsibility to seek help from the signaller to protect his train. I was not opposed to change and modernisation but, not only were the railways getting two jobs for the price of one, safety seemed to be thrown out of the proverbial window.

For this drastic change in working practices, where the driver was being asked to take on the role of guard as well as his own, we were given an extra eight pounds a week on a weekly rate of £146, and £6.63 for each turn worked on our own. With the open station situation, it wouldn't be long before problems with the unruly element of society started to raise their ugly heads.

In the year 1990, after two decades service with the railways, I received a second badge from ASLEF, this time to commemorate my twenty years with the driver's union. Not long after, a position for a Panel Relief Traincrew Inspector became vacant, initially being required to cover holidays and to assist with the catching up with the office paperwork. I duly applied and was successful in my application and, although the job was meant to be on a temporary basis, I covered the position for about four years. When I first started to use the work's computer, everything was done under the old-fashioned MS-DOS system. This took me ages to get used to, but got the hang of it in the end.

My general duties as a relief inspector were to deal with the welfare of the drivers based at Bishop's Stortford depot and generally perform assessment rides with them to see that the railway standards were being maintained. I also became involved in some office work, and was asked if I could come up with a design for a smaller Sectional Appendix (A5 instead of the old A4). These appendices gave drivers most of the relevant basic information about a route, ranging from station mileages, crossing names, and which level crossings had telephones and so on. In the end, I drew up some new Route Maps for drivers to use when either learning a new route, or for reference when refreshing a route where they had not driven for over six months. My route booklets contained bridge numbers, gradient profiles and signal numbers, whereas the Sectional Appendix didn't. I drew most of the north-east London routes that were relevant to our depot in booklet form, and requested that I extended my own knowledge to include the Cambridge to King's Lynn route to be able to benefit Cambridge drivers as well, but this was declined. Only a few of these booklets were released

The 20-year membership badge issued to me by ASLEF is shown on the left.

On the left, is the logo used by Prism Rail, whilst on the right is the new logo introduced for the West Anglia Great Northern Railway.

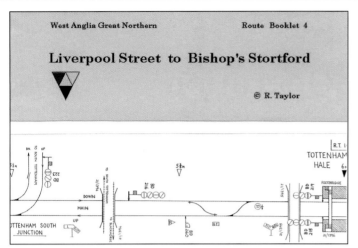

West Anglia Great Northern   Route Booklet 4

Liverpool Street to Bishop's Stortford

© R. Taylor

One of my route booklets, showing the cover and the kind of information that was helpful to drivers when learning a new route. Their actual size was 212mm long by 68mm. The information was relevant in 1990.

before a new version of our Sectional Appendix was eventually produced in an A5 format.

During this same period, trials were made with a Minder Driver concept. Volunteers were required to assist with new trainees, with experienced drivers passing on their knowledge within the driving cab. The original idea was to have the trainee teamed up with a regular driver, and in the first week was to observe how the driver handled his train while learning the route over which he was to end up driving trains. In the second week with the driver, after having received formal training on the particular traction type, the trainee was allowed to actually drive the train, under strict supervision from the driver. Many drivers disliked this new idea and voiced opinions that the practice was unsafe, yet they failed to realise that this practice had been taking place unofficially for years, with drivers letting their secondmen have a drive now and then. In the end, it was recognised that to be able to carry out these new minding duties professionally, formal training was required. In taking on this role, I was able to acquire a City & Guilds Certificate for instructional techniques in March of 1996. Overall, I managed to pass on my experience to thirteen aspiring drivers from Bishop's Stortford and Chingford depots.

Whilst carrying out the Relief Inspector's duties, I was still required to drive trains now and then, and one particular Sunday I encountered a problem that was to eventually lead to my being removed from the Panel Inspector's position. In the early part of 1994, the Stansted Express services were experiencing a few problems, what with the catering service being temporarily removed and the cleaning of some trains being inadequate. Some of the trains were receiving additional stops, and this resulted in a local press report stating that the service was not living up to its 'express' promises. A local passenger service group chairman had questioned the 'express' in Stansted Express, as the service was becoming a stopping train. This led to an internal memo where the Stansted Express team was urged to do everything possible to ensure the smooth running of the service.

Imagine my surprise then, on the Sunday in question, when I was in Liverpool Street station waiting to work an express service to Stansted Airport. These services were always busy, with people flying home after a week-end in London. Just before I was due to depart, I was asked to stop at additional stations because a previous Cambridge service had been cancelled. My booked stops for this train were Tottenham Hale, for connections with the London Underground Victoria

Line, then Bishop's Stortford and Stansted Airport, with a total running time of 42 minutes for the 37 miles. I was then being asked to stop all stations from Waltham Cross to the airport due to the Cambridge cancellation. I objected to this initially, stating that the 322 units were not designed for stop-start all-stations running, but was prepared to compromise by stopping additionally at Broxbourne and Harlow Town. My first thoughts were for the passengers wanting to catch flights from Stansted Airport, knowing that some airlines only had minimal checking-in times. The stranded Cambridge line passengers at least had another service within 20 minutes of my departure. The station managers mulled this over and the compromise was accepted, to the point that these revised stops were advertised to the public. My booked departure time was then delayed by 10 minutes while senior managers debated whether I ought to be stopping all of the stations as they first requested. As a result, I had to attend an interview with my area manager at Broxbourne to explain my actions a few days later. When I put my case forward regarding passengers possibly missing flights due to the extra eight stops and possibly claiming compensation, the manager replied that it wasn't a problem because they were prepared to take any compensation claims to Court. I was disgusted at this lack of concern for paying passengers, and because I dared argue the point, was put back to driving duties permanently!

This wasn't the first time that I had disagreements with some of the management. On one occasion in the 1980s, I had to travel to Broxbourne to pick up my train due to out-of-course running of services. When I arrived there, my slam-door unit was nowhere to be seen so I made enquiries with train control. I was then informed that the train was in a siding about a ¼ mile down the line. I told them that there was no way that I was putting myself at risk by walking along the line with my back to oncoming traffic to get this unit, as there was no recognised safe walking route. The station manager used some initiative by using the Hertford goods locomotive to fetch the electric unit from the siding concerned, only to find that half of the six-car train was 'dead' with its pantograph down. I then refused to take the train into service in this condition, and was sent over to the manager's office to report my actions, then sent back to my depot. I argued that I could not take a train into service where I could not fully prepare the unit, especially with a platform in the way preventing me from seeing the lower half of the train. The manager replied that they would have accepted responsibility for anything that might have been 'hanging off', but I couldn't see this happening in real life. It was always the driver's job to see that the train was fit for public use.

I preferred to work on the Stansted Express services, not least because there were other staff on the train as well. These were the revenue collectors and the catering staff. An additional perk was the odd cup of coffee from the refreshment trolley. The stopping patterns were also quite simple, usually calling at Tottenham Hale, Harlow Town or Bishop's Stortford and Stansted Airport, and vice versa. When given a clear run, speeds of 90mph could be reached in the Broxbourne Junction area on the way to the Airport. Although originally 42 minutes were allowed for the trip from Liverpool Street to Stansted Airport, with a clear run it was possible to complete the run in about 38 minutes, except for the stop at Bishop's Stortford. On a Sunday service, it was possible to arrive at Bishop's Stortford about five minutes early, mainly because there were no other trains to get in the way. Eventually the 42 minute allowance was extended to 45 minutes, because the line capacity was full. This meant that, unless trains were sidetracked at Harlow Town or Broxbourne, the express services caught up with the stopping services in the Cheshunt area.

The 322 units spent a colourful life, changing their original green-stripe livery for a yellow stripe along the bodysides. A

I was disgusted at this lack of concern for paying passengers and because I dared argue the point, was put back to driving duties permanently.

One of the dedicated fleet of 322 units is seen at platform 5 at Liverpool Street in a revised livery of a yellow body-side stripe replacing the original green one. The sharp-eyed among you may notice the Speedy Gonzales mascot sitting in the front window.

Units 481 and 484 stand side by side at the stops in Liverpool Street whilst working Stansted Airport services. The blue livery is of North Western Trains, the unit having been on loan to them for some time.

One of the original 700-series 317s, above, in the darker-blue livery used for the Stansted Express fleet, is seen here in platform 1 at Liverpool Street waiting to work to the airport. Note the bullhead track in platform 2.

The unique experimental-liveried 317 729 at Stansted Airport, waiting to work a service to London Liverpool Street.

handful were leased to North Western Trains for a time to cope with unit shortages in that area. When they came back, they wore a dark blue livery that had large gold stars on the side. The 322 fleet were eventually permanently transferred north to Scotrail/Strathclyde services, where their livery changed to maroon and cream. More recently, the Stansted Express services have been taken over by dedicated 317s in the 700 series, after the 322s were transferred to Scotland. The 317/7 fleet were air-conditioned units and came in a dark metallic-blue colour scheme. These units had a built-in catering galley in each driving trailer. In time, the colour scheme of these units was lightened slightly and one unit, 317 729, came in a one-off metallic-grey livery with orange stripes at the ends of the coaches.

Quite a few of the electric units were stored at Chingford during the day, where they were cleaned and made ready for the evening rush hour. By this stage the trains were either 315s or 317s. The 317s were divided into two types, 317/1 and 317/2. The Mk.1

A line-up of units sitting in the yard at Chingford. The unit on the left is a 315 unit in the purple WAGN colours, while 317 307 is bearing the colours of the LTS railway, where the unit was transferred for a short period. The next unit is one of the Mk II non air-conditioned versions of the 317 fleet. Note the smoother roof line above the cab.

One of the Mk.1 versions of the 317 fleet, in Network SouthEast colours, sits at Hertford East soon after the introduction of these units on the Hertford via Seven Sisters route. In the centre-left of the picture are the run-round points used by locomotive-hauled trains arriving in platform one. The centre road and the points have since been removed.

A panoramic view of the carriage sidings at Chingford, where units were stored in readiness for the rush-hour services. Note the searchlight signals on the end of the platform on the right-hand side of the picture which were eventually changed for three-aspect types.

111

Left: A copy of the Long Service Award Certificate, issued to me for completing 25 years of service.

Below: The 30-year ASLEF badge presented to me by the then Assistant General Secretary, Tony West, also an ex-Stratford driver.

The station master's house at Bishop's Stortford station that eventually became the driver's signing-on point and mess room. The old mess room facilities can be seen on the first floor at the far right of the picture.

versions were air-conditioned, and the external difference was noted by the boxy arrangement over the end vestibule gangway door and the small 'slit-like' ventilators above the bodyside windows. In the summertime, passengers were often tempted to open these small ventilators in the mistaken belief that it would improve the internal air temperature. Unfortunately, this was thermostatically controlled, therefore opening the small 'slits' had no effect whatsoever. The driver had no control over this at all, but this did not stop one commuter complaining to a local village magazine, calling drivers idiots for supposedly switching on the heat on purpose to annoy commuters!

Whilst on the subject of commuters, I found that some of their behaviour could be rather amusing. Being creatures of habit, they would stand in their regular position on the platform like they did every day, then, when the train rolled into the platform, something would overcome them. They would start to dart around all over the place like someone possessed. Some people would casually stroll down the platform as if it were a Sunday afternoon, then when the doors were being closed would rant and rave that they wanted to get on the train. If we waited at stations for every intending traveller, or heeded every "Hang on mate!", we would probably arrive at our final destination about half an hour late. Yet these were the very people that would become indignant if the train arrived at their station about three minutes late!

There was many an occasion that commuters showed me their new watches. In times of disruption, a small minority would turn into the most selfish bunch of people you could ever wish to meet, and would demand that you magic them up a train immediately! Never mind the other few hundred people

A view at Cambridge showing the new 'ONE' livery applied to a class 317 EMU of the 600 series while waiting to work back to London. The old WAGN purple livery is seen on the unit in the background.

When there were shortages of 317s, 315 units sometimes made it to Cambridge. A double set is seen here in platform three at Cambridge on a rather overcast day. The journey from Liverpool Street to Cambridge on one of these units must have been uncomfortable, without any toilet facilities being available on board.

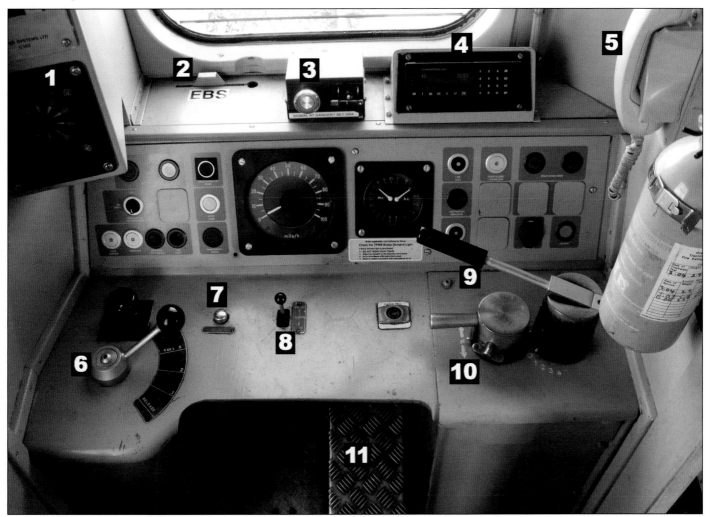

The cab view of a refurbished 315 unit. The controls are as follows:- 1, AWS indicator; 2, Emergency Bypass Switch; 3, Driver's Reminder Appliance (for red signals); 4, Cab Radio; 5, Radio handset; 6, Westcode five-step brake handle; 7, AWS Cancellation button; 8, Horn lever; 9, Power Controller and Driver's Safety Device handle; 10, Reverser handle; 11, D.S.D. foot pedal.

that might want to get home as well. I appreciate that a lot of people's season tickets were rather expensive, but it didn't give them the excuse to abuse railway staff.

The driver was increasingly becoming an ambassador for the railway, and was encouraged to be more 'customer' focussed. Our duties included making on-train announcements and generally helping the travelling public where our train schedules permitted. At one stage, there was a memo requesting drivers to clean trains at terminal stations by picking up papers and taking away rubbish where no staff were provided, as well as filling water tanks and washing the cab windscreen. This demand was soon shelved after further uproar from the driver's union. We were meant to use our judgement while preparing trains, to make sure that they were fit for public use. The trouble was, if both toilets (where provided) were found to be blocked, we were still asked to take the train into service, even though this did not strictly break any rules. The focus now was to keep the service running at all costs, no matter what state the trains were in. After all, we were now part of a business venture, not a public service, and there were performance figures to worry about. This was driven home to us with the issuing of a league table of how much it cost someone to have a train delayed or cancelled. To delay a train on the Bishop's Stortford to Cambridge line by one minute during peak times cost Railtrack £266, or £5,324 for the cancellation of a service.

I preferred to work on outer suburban services like the Stansted Express or the Cambridge trains. At least on the Cambridge services there was plenty of interesting scenery to be seen, instead of up and down to Enfield or Chingford three or four times. The most drawn-out jobs were working the stopping services to Hertford East *via* Seven Sisters. This would involve stopping at 19 stations in each direction, and if one was unfortunate to have three round trips in a day's work, you were glad to see the end of the shift! It was on the inner suburban services that most trouble was encountered, from the unruly element of the non-fare-paying 'customer'. It was surprising to what lengths people would go to avoid paying a £1.50 fare!

In the November of 1995, I was presented with a certificate at a function held at Stevenage, in appreciation of my 25 years of service with the railways. At around the same time, the driver's mess room and associated administration offices at Bishop's Stortford were moved from the location near the round tower, into the ex-Station Master's house on platform one.

In May of the year 2000, I was presented with my thirty-year ASLEF long service badge from the Assistant General Secretary, Tony West who was an ex-Stratford driver himself. ASLEF was behind some of the changes to our West Anglian working practices, most notably the introduction of a 35-hour four-day working week. This gave us two guaranteed days off each week as well as the odd Sunday, but there was an option of working these Rest Days as overtime if one wanted. It stood to reason that this meant the average working day would be in the region of 8½ hours and sometimes more. In the end, we were working some days that lasted nine hours and 55 minutes, if thrown in with a short day of only seven hours. In time, ASLEF would be fighting to 'bring down the hours', claiming that drivers were working excessive hours. A few years later, in 2004, I became disillusioned with ASLEF and withdrew my membership. This once great union seemed to be going off on a political tangent by supporting minority groups, instead of supporting train drivers whilst they were at work. There was political in-fighting regarding the election of a new General Secretary which the membership had voted for, only for this vote to be overturned by the Executive Committee; hardly democratic!

In 2004, the franchise to run the Greater Anglia area was won by the bus company National Express. The name they chose to operate under was 'ONE', which was an acronym for Operated

by National Express. This meant that the whole area of East Anglia was now back under the control of one operator, similar to the days when British Rail were in charge, except only the trains were owned by 'ONE', with the infrastructure being owned and maintained by Railtrack (later to become Network Rail). A new colour scheme was slowly introduced on all of the rollingstock, which could only be described as unusual.

As time passed by, I was becoming more and more disillusioned with my job as a train driver. This was caused by the ever-increasing yobbish behaviour of the ticket-less travelling public on suburban services. This behaviour was made possible by the lack of station staff and on-board revenue collecting personnel and this, in turn, was brought about by cost-cutting exercises or the staff not wanting to expose themselves to unruly behaviour late at night. More often than not, this meant that the only person left to deal with problems was the train driver. The following pages are taken from actual incident reports that I had filed over the years and are in alphabetical order, and show what kind of things that the drivers had to cope with on their own.

Assaults and Muggings

In October 1994, I was working an up Hertford service that called at Clapton at 15:20 in the afternoon. Two middle-aged passengers alighted from the front coach while two younger people got out nearer the rear of the train. One of the younger males made a sprint for the exit and this made one of the first passengers to step back to allow him access to the stairs. I closed my doors and was just about to pull out of the station when someone pulled the emergency cord. Two men alighted and made their way to the front of the train and indicated that one of them had been mugged by the two young blokes who had by now left the premises. It transpired that one of the mugged men had something stolen from him while in transit between Tottenham Hale and Clapton. His friend intervened and was punched on the nose for his trouble. The two thieves had, in fact, joined the train at Tottenham Hale; one of them running down the up escalator to reach the platform as my train had run in.

On the 23rd December 1995, I was the driver rostered to work the 16:32 service from Liverpool Street to Enfield Town. My stopping pattern was semi-fast, which meant that I only stopped at Bethnal Green, Hackney Downs, Stoke Newington, Seven Sisters, White Hart Lane, Silver Street, Edmonton Green, Bush Hill Park and Enfield Town. Due to football having been played at White Hart Lane, I had an eight-car train instead of the usual four-car. When I pulled into Stoke Newington, I had to stop right against the tunnel wall at the far end of the platform to be able to fit the entire length of the train into the platform, as the platform only just held eight coaches. When I released the doors, a passenger alighted from the from the very rear of the train, so I watched his movements on the TV monitor to make sure he was on the main part of the platform. Out of the corner of my eye, I noticed two male youths run from the second coach towards the stairs to the exit. They seemed to be running in panic, and my instincts made me wonder whether they had done something wrong. I paused before closing the doors, half expecting someone to stick their head out of the train to report something amiss. As no-one did, I closed the doors and proceeded to my next booked stop, Seven Sisters.

On arriving there, a lady passenger asked me to call an ambulance as a man had been hit over the head with a bottle and that there was lots of blood on the floor! I called for the ambulance, found the gentleman wandering along the platform and took him to the station-staff rest room for some first-aid attention. He was able to tell me that he was minding his own business when two youths came walking through the train

This once great union seemed to be going off on a political tangent by supporting minority groups, instead of supporting train drivers whilst they were at work

114

Arrogant people such as these two from Turkey Street used to take great delight in delaying the train while they casually held conversations with their mates on board the train.

Two trespassers seen wandering beside the track near Ponders End, apparently helping to clear away some timber posts.

and one said "Alright mate? Have a merry Christmas," and with that was hit on the head with a bottle. He had not spoken to or intimidated them in any way, and their motive did not appear to be robbery, as they had taken nothing from him. The poor man had suffered a gash on his forehead above his left eye and a scratch from the middle of his forehead to the top of his nose. On returning to Liverpool Street, the train was taken out of service for forensic investigation by the British Transport Police.

Soon after incidents such as these, and one where a driver was threatened with a knife on attempting to reset a communication cord, at a special meeting of the Bishop's Stortford and Chingford branches of ASLEF, a new resolution was adopted. It stated that as from 23:00 on 2nd July 1996, no suburban service would be worked unless an additional member of staff was provided. For a short while the Company did provide security staff, but these were not effective because they were not given powers of arrest. More often than not, they hid at the rear of the train to 'keep out of trouble'!

Delays

Sometimes, a certain amount of delay during busy times is inevitable during a train journey, but it used to infuriate me when other delays could have been avoided. This particular report involved the Stansted Express service being delayed unnecessarily, when the signal box was still operational at Bishop's Stortford. Shortly after leaving Stansted Airport with the 07:00 service to London, I was brought to a stand by a red signal just outside of the Tye Green portal of the airport tunnel. Before I could contact the signaller, the red light turned to green. Later in the journey, I caught up with a stopping service at Brimsdown and had to follow this train all the way to Tottenham Hale. After this, I was brought to a stand at Clapton Junction while a Down Chingford service trundled by. When we eventually passed through Hackney Downs station, we ran parallel with an Up Enfield service that was booked to run all stations, but guess who got the green light at Bethnal Green North Junction? I was due into London at 07:45 and was then supposed to uncouple the two units and leave at 08:00 with a four-car express back to the airport. Considering that I didn't arrive until 07:56, there was no way that we were going to leave on time. Drivers were always being pestered with memos about having to be in their cabs at least five minutes before they were due away, and I complained that it would help if signallers did their job more efficiently. As if to reinforce this point, later in the same day I had left Liverpool Street on time with the 10:00 express airport service, only to be held at Bethnal Green for two-and-a-half minutes while an Up slow service rolled over the junction in front of me. If I had been given a clear run, it would have taken me only fifty seconds to have cleared Bethnal Green North Junction. The reasons behind this were the fact that movements of trains in and out of Liverpool Street were

computer-controlled under a system known as Automatic Route Setting, the acronym of which is quite appropriate. This meant that trains were run in the strict order that the Working Time Table set down, irrespective of whether a train was late or not.

Sometimes delays were caused by arrogant people standing in the train doorways casually holding conversations with other people. This could cause up to three or four minutes to be lost, especially if the people concerned forced the issue by making the driver get out of his cab to 'have a word'.

Drunks

One night, I had an incident at Waltham Cross where a passenger was half in and half out of a set of doors towards the rear of the 00:02 service from Liverpool Street to Bishop's Stortford. After making two requests for him to stand clear of the doors, he then pulled the communication cord. I went back to investigate and found an intoxicated male stating that he was stuck in the doors, and he then started brandishing a device that was used to pick up litter. I reset the cord, made my way to the front, only to find that the cord had been pulled again, so I summoned the Police. He was beginning to annoy some people in the first-class section and things were getting nasty. Suddenly, another drunken person grabbed the litter-picker, bent it into a nice 'Z' shape, and told the other drunk where to go in no uncertain terms. He eventually left the train, so we departed before he had a chance to board the train again. I never did see any sign of the Police and, to this day do not know whether they turned up or not.

General Interruptions

What follows happened in one particular week in March of 2000. Some of these incidents I reported and others I didn't. If I reported everything that I considered out of the ordinary upon the railway, I would be permanently at a desk writing reports. At the beginning of this particular week, I saw a man dressed in orange overalls at the side of the track between Seven Sisters and Stamford Hill on the Up Enfield line. As I whistled to warn him of my approach, his response was to drop a sleeper that he had been fiddling with, turn his back to me and look sheepish and otherwise occupied. As he didn't acknowledge my whistle, I presumed that he wasn't a railwayman but someone attempting to steal a sleeper, as there was a white van parked nearby. When I arrived in London, I discovered that children had attempted to set fire to seats in the rear coach.

The next two incidents involve trespass, which was becoming so common it was laughable. There are some people who treat the railway as a public footpath, oblivious of the danger imposed by passing trains travelling at 80 miles per hour. Once my written reports filtered through the system it was far too late, with 'lack of resources' as the usual response. The first instance was when I noticed two young boys climbing up from a footpath underbridge in Edmonton, to gain access to the station.

The second occasion happened two stations up the line on the same service, where two males were found walking along the track. When I sounded the whistle, they both dived for cover. I reported these incidents at Seven Sisters, and when I arrived in London, was met by two British Transport Police officers, who then accompanied the train back as far as White Hart Lane on my way to Enfield Town. When I returned from Enfield, the doors were forced open by two schoolboys as the train entered Bush Hill Park station, which brought me to an abrupt halt. The on-board 'security' person made no attempt to come forward to investigate, preferring to remain in the safety of the rear of the train. We then picked up the two Police officers at White Hart Lane, and half of the train decided to disembark!

Later in the week, two youths came up to my cab at Hackney Downs, and I thought they were about to ask a question. One of them suddenly thrust something in my face and clicked it twice. I flinched, not knowing whether it was a gun, a flick knife or something else. It turned out to be a cigarette lighter, and because I flinched, they thought it was a great joke and went off laughing. I was just leaving the platform with my train and did not report the incident, even though I was shook up by the event, as I considered it would be a waste of time. By the time anyone with authority turned up, they would have been long gone. I also did not want to delay the train, chasing after nonentities.

My next working involved the 16:41 train to Chingford. This train was also brought to a stand by people forcing open the doors, and I came to an abrupt halt about ¾ mile from Chingford station. I opened my side door on the 315 unit and noticed six youths running back down the track towards a footpath underbridge. They obviously lived nearby and were too lazy to walk all the way from Chingford station. This was a common problem when working with 315 units, as a two minute time-delay was fitted only to these units, supposedly to eliminate stress to the bogie frames if drivers used the emergency position on the brake handle too often. ASLEF tried to get this time delay removed, as many drivers were frustrated at being brought to a stand by the mindless element of the travelling public, then having to wait two minutes before the brakes would release. The time delay feature still exists on these units to this day. After reporting these incidents to one of my managers at Chingford, stating that I had had enough for one day, I was told that we have to accept this kind of antisocial behaviour these days. I totally disagreed. Why bother to have Bye-Laws if they are never enforced?

Level Crossing Incidents
Level crossings in general are safe, if used correctly, but many drivers have encountered incidents where level crossings were abused by cars dodging around half barriers. One near-miss that I had, involved a farm crossing between Audley End and Great Chesterford on the way to Cambridge with the 15:19 from Liverpool Street. The crossing is approached on a long left-hand curve and, from a distance, I had noticed that the self-worked barriers were up, so as a precaution, I started to reduce speed from about 73 miles per hour. When the crossing came into clear view, a crop-sprayer tractor crossed from right to left in front of my train and I was able to bring my train to a stand at the crossing. Had I been travelling at the line speed of 80 miles per hour, I would have most certainly hit the vehicle, as I usually use the crossing as a braking point on the approach to Great Chesterford station. It transpired that the tractor driver had not even bothered to use the telephone provided for his own safety.

Objects on the Line
From time to time, it was not unusual to find objects placed deliberately on the track, usually by bored children during their school holidays. Most often, the objects were pieces of ballast placed upon the rails and the children were rather amused to see a train crush these pieces of stone as it passed by at speed. Sometimes the objects were slightly larger, with the sole intention of trying to derail the train.

The most unusual 'object' I encountered was while I was working a train between Bishop's Stortford and Cambridge. On my first trip, I was cautioned by the Cambridge signaller just before reaching Newport in Essex. He advised me that some cattle had been reported on or near the line in the vicinity of Newport station, and I was to travel through the area at caution and advise him accordingly as to whether I encountered any of the bovine creatures. This was most unusual, as the farming in the area was mostly agricultural, with some sheep seen now and then, but rarely cows. I completed the trip to Cambridge and back to Bishop's Stortford without any problems. At 'Stortford, I was due to have my tea break, then work another trip to Cambridge and back before I finished duty. The stops on this second trip were to be Audley End, Whittlesford and then Cambridge. I was not cautioned on this trip, so it was fair to assume that the cattle problem had been cleared up, although we are trained on this job never to assume anything. With this in mind, I reduced speed in the area where the stray cattle had been reported, just in case, as the sun was setting and daylight was fading fast.

With nothing to be found at Newport, I accelerated the train towards Audley End and saw something on the line ahead. At first glance, it appeared as if it was a person looking for these stray cattle, so I sounded the horn. As I drew closer at about sixty-five mile an hour, the object moved and I instantly realised that it was the rear end of a cow! It was too late to be able to stop and the poor animal met its maker. As we were on a left-hand curve, my fear was that we were about to be derailed, and I had visions of the train careering over the viaduct that crosses what was the old A11 road. We eventually came to a stand on the bridge over this road and, after informing the passengers and signaller of the circumstances, went back to check what damage had been done to the unit. I half expected to find some of the wheels derailed, but the only evident damage was to a control box under my cab known as the Drum Switch. This was pushed back by about 90° but other than that, everything was fine. We were able to carry on to Cambridge, where we arrived about thirty minutes late.

Track Defects
The driver was always being told that they were they 'eyes and ears' for the Company, and if we ever saw anything that was considered unsafe, we were to report it straight away. One instance of this springs to mind regarding a misaligned rail joint I had noticed after some weekend engineering work. A new rail had been bolted to an old rail and resulted in a severe jolt as the train passed from old rail to new rail. I was stopped at the very location by a red signal, so with the signalman's knowledge I took a closer look. What I found horrified me, so I informed the signalman straight away. The profile of the old rail was so worn that there was a ½" difference between that and the new rail. I suggested that a ten-mile-an-hour speed restriction ought to be imposed immediately, as it posed a derailment risk.

A close-up view of the misaligned track joint that was reported by me. Look how worn the old rail was!

The picture above shows the alignment of the mismatched rail joints, looking in the direction of travel. With trains traveling at thirty miles an hour on this curve, with the close proximity of the points, I considered it to be a derailment risk without the imposition of a severe speed restriction.

The signalman reassured me that the permanent-way staff would be informed straight away. The joint was on a 30 mile-an-hour left-hand curve preceding a set of points, and was on a busy section of line used by Cambridge and Stansted Airport services as well as the Chingford suburban trains. The following day there seemed to be little improvement with the ride over this joint, so I made enquiries with the signalman again. He stated that the joint had been inspected and ground down to improve the ride. The photograph above shows this joint after the grinding 'improvement', and the misalignment was still evident.

I had not received any response to my written reports whatsoever, so I reported the matter via an internal confidential reporting system known as CIRAS. The answer I received from this quarter was just as bad, as the people who were ultimately responsible for the infrastructure misunderstood the misalignment report, mistaking it for a vertical fault instead of a lateral one. In the light of this, they reported that there was no derailment risk. It made me wonder whether anyone had physically inspected the bad joint in the first place! The old rail in this location was eventually renewed nearly eighteen months later!

Unusual occurrences

Prior to leaving Stansted Airport on the 14th October 2000 with the 17:30 departure, I had heard some thunder in the area. The weather had just turned showery from about 16:55 and was fairly localised. We departed on time and after I had travelled about 600 yards into the tunnel, all of the tunnel lights came on. This can be an indication that another train has entered the tunnel from the opposite direction, and, fearing that a Down train had slid past the signal protecting the other end of the tunnel, I brought my train to a halt, as per laid-down instructions. As I was stopping, the signal in the middle of the tunnel changed from green to a yellow, and at the same time, all of the tunnel lights went out as well as my headlight. The train came to a stand right in the middle of the mile-long tunnel. I came to the conclusion that there must have been a lightning strike in the area, so I attempted an Emergency Call on the cab radio. After a slight pause, the radio responded with 'Emergency -No Answer'! I informed the passengers over the PA system about the possible cause for our loss of overhead power, then left the cab to contact the Bishop's Stortford signaller by the means of a trackside telephone, as my mobile phone did not work within the confines of the tunnel. The signalman confirmed that there had been a lightning strike that had affected the whole area, but couldn't give a timescale as to how long things would be before they could be restored back to normal. At least he was able to switch on the tunnel's emergency lights.

I informed the passengers that it might be some considerable time until the power was restored, but that they were quite safe where they were. The inevitable questions from passengers weren't long in coming, "How long are we likely to be?" and "Can't we go back to the Airport?" being the two favourites. After liaising with the on-board hosts, we decided to hand out tea and coffee to keep people occupied. One of the hostesses came forward to inform me that a lady in the fourth coach was claustrophobic and, getting agitated, had started to panic. I made the decision to escort her from the train to prevent her 'nerves' from spreading to others. I arranged for a hostess to accompany me and the three people concerned, complete with luggage, whilst I left another host in charge of the train. (Luckily there was more than one on board!) I informed the signalman of what we were about to do, and asked him to make arrangements to have these passengers met at the Tye Green portal and taken forward by road.

Once we reached the London-end of the tunnel, 900 metres later, I left the hostess to look after the passengers, making sure that no-one wandered from their position of safety. I contacted the signalman again, and he informed me that airport staff were on their way by road. When I returned to my stranded train, I learned that there was an asthmatic male passenger who was possibly on the verge of an attack at the rear of the train. The hostess was asking, *via* the cab-to-cab intercom, whether the man could stand on the tunnel platform for some 'fresher' air, but she didn't know how to release the rear cab door. I walked back the length of the eight-car train to allow the gentleman access to the platform, and the hostess told me that none of the on-board staff were trained on how to evacuate a train or how to work the doors in case of an emergency. I found that piece of news quite shocking and, after the event, made a recommendation that all airport staff should be trained on how to carry out train evacuations.

By this stage, one or two passengers were pressing for a total evacuation, but I persuaded them that they were safer where they were until I was informed otherwise. At least we were in the dry, whereas it was still pouring with rain outside in the descending darkness. Eventually, after 1½ hours, the power was restored and we were able to make a move to the tunnel exit with the signalman's permission. As I drew near to the tunnel opening to pick up the hostess that I had left there, I noticed that everyone that I had left were still there! It transpired that the staff from the airport got lost in trying to locate the tunnel mouth! I apologised profusely to everyone and helped them back onto the train. After a fairly uneventful run, we made it to Liverpool Street at about 19:50.

A lot of drivers that day helped out by putting in extra hours beyond their normal call of duty. Managers also did their bit by rescuing trapped trains and ferried customers in their own cars! Exceptional work by all under extremely difficult circumstances

Vandalism

On running into Stamford Hill on the way up to London at about 21:10 one evening with a stopping service from Cheshunt, I noticed a group of youths at the very end of the platform near the rear of my train. They boarded the train in the rear coach. At our next station, Stoke Newington, the youths alighted - the last one spraying a foam fire extinguisher all over the place. They ran up the staircase near the back of the train and the now empty fire extinguisher came sailing over the bridge wall, landing on the platform. Choosing discretion as the better part of valour, I carried on to the next station where I went back to see if there had been any damage done to train or passengers. The fire extinguisher had been squirted around the interior of the coach. When I entered the rear cab lobby, I noticed that both of the driver's cab windows had been smashed with a large foam fire extinguisher, which was laying on the floor. The small extinguisher had been stolen. As I made my way back to the front of the train, I was met by a passenger who had been in the coach when the havoc was being created. He had been sprayed all over his back with the extinguisher. The event was reported to the signaller and I requested Police presence for my next trip back down the same line. As this couldn't be provided (lack of resources), I booked off duty there and then, considering it too unsafe to take the 22:20 service back to Enfield.

When I changed ends one day, after working the 16:35 from Enfield, I noticed a burning smell from within the last vehicle. Someone had attempted to set fire to newspapers on some of the seats, causing scorch marks on the seat material and the floor. From the position in the train, I could say with certainty that this damage was caused by school children who normally join the train at Edmonton and alight (no pun intended) at Hackney Downs. Considering that the fire extinguishers were continually being tampered with or stolen, it was a very dangerous situation to be in. Again, there was no security staff in attendance on the train.

After the cab-smashing incident, I wrote a letter to one of my managers, stating that it appeared that circumstances were becoming too dangerous to expect drivers to protect the travelling public and ourselves on our own! I had had enough of having passengers being intimidated, mugged, sprayed with fire extinguishers, and the trains being wrecked and set on fire! After having to suffer numerous humiliating occasions of waiting two minutes for the brakes to release when doors were forced open, drivers were losing their patience. It seemed ridiculous to have Bye Laws in place when it was impossible to enforce them. Soon after this, attempts were made to utilise security staff on trains that were known to suffer regular problems and for a while, things did improve.

Train drivers are faced with the unruly element of society nearly every day, not just at weekends any more. Take one of our local stations in the village of Stansted Mountfitchet for example. Commuters in the evening have to regularly endure being intimidated or even jostled by the under-age drunk youths that hang around the station there. The amount of vandalism and mindless behavior that has taken place at this quiet little station defies belief. Young people think nothing of climbing onto the station canopy, within feet of twenty-five thousand volt electric overhead cables, or casually crossing the tracks by jumping off the platform instead of using the footbridge, especially while under the influence of alcohol or drugs. Being on a slight curve, the consequences here don't bear thinking about, as Stansted Express services hurtle through this station at 70 miles per hour! Some think it is ultra cool to stand on the platform edge with their toes hanging off the white line, while a train passes by. They have been known to play football by kicking the ball from one platform to the other, smashing anything that resembles glass, vandalising the picket fence to use as weapons, and leaving their drug-taking paraphernalia laying around for the staff to find in the morning. Bottles can always be found smashed up all over the place, as well as dumped food from the local take-aways. The station brickwork was slowly being demolished, with some of the loosened masonry being hurled at passing trains. Poster frames had been ripped from the station walls and placed on the track for trains to run over, and cars and bicycles were regularly damaged. The mindless few also found time to interfere with the cameras and monitors that were used by drivers for observing passengers alighting from trains.

There are some people in society that think this kind of behaviour is just the young expressing themselves. A local councillor considered that perhaps if the place was given a new facelift with a coat of paint, things would improve. I had to point out to him that the only thing that the kids would be admiring would be their names that they scratched onto the nice clean surfaces. When these matters have been reported to the Police, politics would get in the way, with the Essex Police claiming that it was a Railway problem, and British Transport Police saying that they were hopelessly understaffed.

Not all was doom and gloom upon the railways. Tall tales and practical jokes abounded amongst railwaymen around the world. A classic one from Australia was the tale about a couple travelling on a slow train somewhere in the Outback. The man kept pestering the guard about their likely arrival at their destination and the guard was becoming a bit impatient. "We'll get there eventually. What's the rush?" The bloke replied that his wife was pregnant and due to give birth, to which the guard replied that she shouldn't have got on the train in that condition. The man replied "When she got on the train, she wasn't in this condition." Another tale involved one of the wayside goods trains on the Adelaide to Port Pirie line, where the guard was responsible for dropping off the occasional package at certain stations. On this particular day, he was supposed to leave a consignment of butter at an unattended station, with strict instructions to leave it in the shade. He did, but in the shade of the train!

In Britain, on some of the late-night hauled services between Liverpool Street and Norwich, passengers would sometimes ask the guard to wake them up just before their stop.

On one occasion, a passenger had asked to be woken just before Colchester. "I'm a heavy sleeper, so just shove me off if you don't get any sense out of me." He gave the guard a quid for his troubles. At Ipswich the passenger came rushing down

A drinks machine placed at Hertford East station for the public's benefit is seen smashed up with its contents missing. Drivers were having to face this kind of environment more and more when working on their own.

This is the kind of thing that drivers are increasingly being confronted with. These two kids were nonchalantly sitting on the edge of the London-bound platform at Edmonton Green, which is on a 40 mph curve. The consequences of a train coming from the other direction while my train was standing in the station don't bear thinking about.

the platform shouting "What's going on? You didn't wake me up!" Later, another passenger commented "He was very irate wasn't he?", to which the guard replied "Yeah, but I bet he's not half as furious as the bloke I threw out at Colchester."

On one occasion, an unfortunate Stratford driver left his bag unattended in the mess room for just a while and when he came back to collect it, wondered why it seemed a lot heavier than normal. When he looked inside, he noticed that a cast iron brake block had been placed in it! Someone else had been unfortunate to leave their plastic cup upon an electric stove in the same mess room and within minutes, someone 'accidentally' turned the stove on.

Stratford has now changed beyond all recognition. The site where the old diesel depot once stood has now become the location for the new Stratford International Channel Tunnel Rail Link. The old freight yards at Temple Mills have been converted to accommodate a new maintenance workshop for the Eurostar trains, as well as new holding sidings that replace the Thornton Fields carriage sidings. That site is now being developed for the 2012 Olympic Stadium. A brand new training academy has also opened for the training of railway staff, utilising state-of-the-art simulators and modern technology, and this is now located off Stratford Broadway. The London Underground Jubilee line now terminates at Stratford, and the Docklands Light Railway now extends to North Woolwich, replacing the line that was run by Silver Link services.

A train driver's job is an interesting one, but shift work does not agree with everybody. Getting up at four o'clock in the morning does have its benefits, in particular having a road to oneself when driving in to work. Sometimes we were lucky to see some spectacular sunrises from within the cab. The pictures on the following pages will give the reader an opportunity to see certain locations that only drivers are privileged to see.

These days, anyone who would like to become a train driver usually has to scour the internet to find a Train Operating Company that has current vacancies. They would then be required to submit an application along with an up-to-date CV. If the initial interview is successful, they will then be required to attend 36 weeks worth of intensive training, which includes a Company Induction course, followed by a three-week Operations Induction course. At the end of this first month, the candidate will then sit through an assessment to see if they are able to continue with the rest of the training. This will then become more complex, involving such things as riding in the cab with a driver, learning more about the core Rules and Regulations, gaining traction knowledge and route learning skills. They will then be required to spend 16 weeks working with a Minder driver whilst they gain the practical skills of actually driving a train, with a minimum period of 240 hours. Long gone are the days of a minimum five-year apprenticeship with a regular driver.

Once upon a time, many a schoolboy wanted to become a train driver. Nowadays a train driver's job is looked at from a totally different perspective. Many a person has left a well-paid job and downshifted to drive trains for a living. Within the industry, it has always been recognised that the driver's job has been well paid compared to other departments and the responsibility and varying shift patterns has a large bearing on this. On the lower end of the scale, the average drivers' wage is now £32,000 a year and the upper level of £40,000 per annum is paid by some companies. The profession is now attracting more and more women into what was once a male domain.

The modern train driver has many roles and responsibilities, but their main purpose is to drive trains in a safe, punctual and economical manner in accordance with the Rules and Regulations. It is now a driver's responsibility to be aware of, and comply with, the Business Standards of their particular Railway Company to enable them to improve customer satisfaction. A

A view from platform 12 at Stratford station overlooking the site that used to house the maintenance depot. Behind this sign is now the site for the new Stratford International station on the Channel Tunnel Rail Link. The space between the Stratford sign and the low relief International station is now being built upon for the 2012 Olympic village.

driver must appear for duty wearing the full uniform provided. It is considered okay to run a train that is covered from floor to ceiling with graffiti, the interior strewn with the public's litter, or both sets of toilets blocked, yet a driver appearing on duty without wearing his tie is considered bad for the company image, as if this will make any difference to the running of the train!

Woe betide any driver who goes sick or feels that he does not meet the exacting standards required of him. He then exposes himself to what is known as the Managing For Attendance procedure. Under this process, drivers are monitored for their attendance levels and three or more breaches can result in being removed from driving or possible dismissal.

Stratford Low Level station in 2008, looking southeast, with the new London Underground Jubilee Line platforms on the right taking up what was once the engineers' sidings.

The driving environment is no longer as relaxed as it used to be, with pressures to keep the trains running on time, but without exceeding speed limits. The driver has much to assimilate, what with ever-changing shift patterns, rule and regulation changes, and modified train stopping patterns. As well as this, a driver is also required to make Public Address announcements on board the train to keep the passengers informed of arrivals at certain stations, as well as information regarding delays. A driver who forgets his stopping pattern, or slips past a red signal, is likely to be breathalysed, and given a 16-page report to fill out, even though the alcohol consumption limit is far stricter than any airline pilot's.

No driver sets out on purpose to pass a signal at danger (known as a SPAD), and it is interesting to see press reports that drivers have 'jumped' a red light, as if we are impatiently waiting for a red light to turn green. As mentioned in previous chapters, railway signals do not work like traffic lights. A common reason for signals passed at danger in the past was the misjudgement of railhead conditions during the leaf fall season in the autumn. This is now becoming less of a problem with the introduction of Multi Purpose Rail Cleaning Vehicles, and the introduction of TPWS at key signals. The regulations for dealing with SPADS are not laid down by the railway itself but by Her Majesty's Railway Inspectorate, who give specific procedures to maintain a safe railway.

Privatisation has a lot to answer for, as it has broken up the railways into too many disaffected departments. A driver may work for a certain Train Operating Company, whereas the controlling signaller will be working for Network Rail. The maintenance of the track will be contracted out by Network Rail to firms who have little railway-engineering knowledge. The main criteria these days are the performance figures, and the blame culture has resurfaced in some departments, because somebody has to pay for the delays and disruptions.

Who wants to be a train driver?

Views from the Cab

Sunrise on a frosty morning at Coppermill Junction, between Tottenham Hale and Clapton. The old goods line was still in use when this picture was taken. The white lights above the green signal are an indication to drivers that they are about to be diverted to the right at the junction ahead.

The same location in 2007, with the goods road having been lifted some years ago and the line to Stratford electrified. The train we are on is a Stansted Airport to Stratford service.

The driver's view whilst standing in platform 1 at Broxbourne waiting for the passing of a Stansted Express service, seen here utilising a non-dedicated 317 unit. Just beyond our red signal can be seen a set of trap-points, once used to divert runaway trains towards the sand drag seen in the middle distance. Nowadays, a Train Protection Warning System is used, the grid of which can be seen in the middle of the track adjacent to the signal.

Still at Broxbourne, but this time looking northeast. The train is about to rejoin the main line from the Down loop. In the top right of the picture is a box with the word 'OFF' illuminated. These were used to assist station staff whenever there was an eight-car train in the platform, so they could tell when the signal was showing a proceed aspect.

The 'US' above the green signal tells us that we are being diverted *via* the Up Southbury line, in this view at Cheshunt station looking towards London.

The view of the Liverpool Street station approach after just exiting from Bishopsgate Tunnel. Worship Street girder bridge can be seen at the top of the picture. Since the building-over of this section in the summer of 2008, this view is now in darkness as well.

Excursion Trains

To celebrate the 125th anniversary of the London Tilbury & Southend Railway, an Intercity 125 train was run into Liverpool Street from Shoeburyness in 1981. The train is seen here arriving at platform 13 at Liverpool Street. The initial LTS services ran from what was known as Bishopsgate Station.

The Class 40 Preservation Society ran this Anglian Diesel Farewell tour with 40 122, otherwise known as D200, in a green livery, to commemorate the end of Class 40 use on British Rail. It is seen here on the 9th May 1987 with train number 1G50, passing the outskirts of Bishop's Stortford.

Preserved English Electric Class 40 locomotive number 40 145 passes through rural Elsenham station on its way to London Liverpool Street with the Class 40 Preservation Society's Silver Jubilee three-day excursion run by Pathfinder Tours on 22nd January 2005. MIKE REA

A Three Counties Steam weekend was held on 17th and 18th of April, 1993, and two locomotives were used, *Duke of Gloucester*, and *Britannia*, seen here passing over the level crossing at Elsenham station. Special manoeuvres of the locomotives were required to turn them and the Stansted Airport triangle and the emergency crossovers at Elsenham were used for this purpose. Bishop's Stortford driver Peter Curtis was the driver on this loco, seen here carrying 'The University City Express' headboard. Other names carried on the trains that weekend were as follows: (Saturday) 'Three Counties Express', 'Lea Valley Enterprise', 'The Stortsman', 'The West Anglian', 'The Ely Belle' and 'The Cathedrals Express'. On Sunday, the names were 'Cecil Rhodes Explorer', 'Herts & Essex Limited', 'Standen Engineering Limited', 'The Croft Quarryman' and 'The Heron Line Limited'.

A picture taken at Stansted Airport on 5th January 2008, after unit 317 714 had suffered at the hands of graffiti 'artists' during the Christmas break of 2007 whilst in the sidings at Bishop's Stortford. This unit had been allowed to run around in this condition for at least 10 days; not good for the 'company image'.

A half-hearted attempt to clean some graffiti on a 315 unit, seen here at Chingford station.

ABOVE: A view of the old driver's depot at Enfield Town, showing the view of the signing-on office soon after its closure. As the brickwork states, a depot has been at this location from 1849 to 1989. R.I.P.

LEFT: On a lighter note, the resident fox of Ilford Carriage Sidings near Seven Kings is seen pausing just for a second to have its picture taken in the middle of the day!

A sorry scene at the Down Yard at Bishop's Stortford one stormy summer's afternoon. The yard had been closed to freight traffic for some time and the aggregate traffic was now using the facilities at Harlow Mill. This site is now earmarked for redevelopment.

Sunset at Stansted Airport.

GLOSSARY
Terms and Abbreviations

ALCO	American Locomotive Company.
A.R.H.S.	Australian Railway Historical Society.
A.S.L.E.F.	Associated Society of Locomotive Engineers & Firemen.
A.W.S.	Automatic Warning System.
Bardic Lamp	Hand lamp used by British train crews.
Barracks	Sleeping quarters used for train crews to take rest whilst working away from home.
B.R.	British Rail.
B.T.H.	British Thompson Houston, (engine type).
B.U.T.	British Universal Traction, (engine type).
C.D.	Close Doors.
Crib	Australian railway-slang term for meal break.
Cross	A train movement on a single line, passing another train travelling in the opposite direction.
C.T.C.	Centralised Traffic Control.
D.C.	Direct current, usually referring to third rail traction supply.
D.M.U.	Diesel Multiple Unit, commonly called a railcar.
D.O.O.	Driver Only Operation.
Down	Direction of rail traffic, away from a main city terminal.
Electric Staff	Metal grooved rod, possession of which allows a train to enter a single line.
E.M.U.	Electric Multiple Unit.
Engineman	Train driver, usually of locomotives.
E.S.R.	Emergency Speed restriction.
E.T.H.	Electric Train Heating.
Fireman	Driver's assistant or secondman. Term carried over from steam traction.
G.E.	Great Eastern (railway).
G.N.	Great Northern (railway).
G.W.R.	Great Western Railway.
Light Engine	Locomotive running without a train.
L.M.S.	London, Midland & Scottish (railway).
L.N.E.R.	London & North Eastern Railway.
L.T.S.	London, Tilbury & Southend (railway).
Motorman	Train Driver, usually of Railcars (Aus.) or Electric Multiple Units.
Off	A term used when a signal is showing a proceed aspect. Derived from. the days when a derail device was taken 'off the track when the line was clear to proceed.
On	A term used to denote that a signal is showing a red aspect. Derived from when a derail device was placed upon a rail to prevent trains entering a blocked line.
Pass	A train movement on a single line that passes another train travelling in the same direction.
P & D	Preparation and disposal of traction units, usually within a depot.
Permanent Way	The track that the trains ran on, sometimes shortened to P-way.
P.N.B.	Physical Needs Break.
P.S.R.	Permanent Speed Restriction.
Railcar	Self-propelled traction unit that has its engine located below floor level (DMU).
R.A.	Right Away, an indication to the driver that station duties are complete and that the train may proceed.
Road (Having the)	Signal that is showing a proceed aspect.
Road (Knowing the)	Having route knowledge over a particular line.
S.A.R.	South Australian Railways.
Signal Cabin	Signal box.
Stick	Australian railway-slang term for signal.
Switch	Points or turnouts, means of changing the line on which a train is travelling on.
Switch Stand	Manual method of operating points, featuring a coloured target and lamp on a 6' high pole (Aus.).
T.O.P.S.	Total Operations Processing System.
T.P.W.S.	Train Protection Warning System.
Up	Direction of rail traffic, towards main city terminal.
W.A.G.N.	West Anglia Great Northern.
W.T.T.	Working Time Table.